PSYCHOLOGY OF SUCCESS
A Positive Approach to Lifelong Learning

Denis Waitley, Ph.D.

Compiled by   *Gloria P. Pasquini*
Carlene M. Timura

Donna J. Yena, Consultant
Johnson & Wales University
Division of Student Success

Vivian Hoglund, Consultant
Director of P.A.R. Motivation and
Retention Division

IRWIN
Homewood, IL 60430
Boston, MA 02116

PSYCHOLOGY OF SUCCESS
A Positive Approach to Lifelong Learning

Copyright © 1990
P.A.R. Incorporated

Book Manufacture	*Banta Company*
Cover Printing	*E. A. Johnson*
Text and Cover Design	*Stephen Eichhorn Design*
Desktop Publishing	*Louise R. Phaneuf*
Senior Editor	*Carol A. Long*

ISBN 0-89702-091-X

4 5 6 BA 6 5 4 3 2

Table of Contents

Foreword

Foreword

*T*he ten qualities you are about to study in this book are basic methods used by successful people in all walks of life. They are a collection of naturally self-imposed characteristics which can be used as a tool for positive lifelong learning. Those qualities are *Positive Self-Direction, Self-Image, Self-Discipline, Self-Motivation, Self-Awareness, Self-Esteem, Self-Projection, Self-Control, Self-Expectancy,* and *Self-Dimension.*

*D*enis Waitley is an Annapolis graduate with advanced degrees in science and psychology and a doctorate degree in human behavior. Through his research and rehabilitation work with the U.S. Viet Nam prisoners of war, motivational training of Super Bowl and Olympic athletes, and simulation work with NASA astronauts, Dr. Waitley observed that these ten attitudinal qualities surfaced again and again. Although each group experienced different victories and defeats, the common thread was the achievement of a goal. The result was his authoring of two books, *The Psychology of Winning* and *The Winner's Edge.* It is the blending of these two best selling books that has given birth to the course you are about to study.

*A*s you study the qualities presented in this textbook, you will find that each one relies upon others to add to its strength and reinforce its purpose of helping you achieve success. No principle is more or less important than the others, and no one quality is solely responsible for successful lifelong learning. It is for this reason that these principles of thought and healthy behavior intertwine.

*W*aitley uses two terms exclusively throughout this textbook. They are *"Winners"* and *"Losers,"* and they are his trademark for instruction. The term Losers refers to those people in our society who "lose out" on life's opportunities because they do not set goals for themselves. They are the people who put themselves down, who would rather follow the crowd than make their own decisions. Their definition of success is always someone else's achievements. Winners, on the other hand, are those individuals who, *"in a very natural, free-flowing way* *seem to get what they want from life. They put themselves together across the board – at school, work, home, in the community, and in society. They set and achieve goals which benefit themselves and others."* It is the major aim of this course to have you stand among the Winners in whatever endeavors you set for yourself.

T here are no bells and whistles. Just ten basic qualities that when assimilated by you, the student, will bring you to the top of every situation you encounter. The main point you must remember when studying *The Psychology of Success: A Positive Approach to Lifelong Learning* is that your *attitude* toward your potential is the key to unlocking the door to personal fulfillment.

Gloria P. Pasquini
Carlene M. Timura

1

POSITIVE SELF-DIRECTION

*No wind blows
in favor of a
ship without a
destination*

---

*If you don't know where
you're going,
you'll probably end up
somewhere else*

AIMS

❖ To identify the differences between the terms *"Winners"* and *"Losers"* as they pertain to *Positive Self-Direction*

❖ To establish short- and long-term goals

❖ To become proficient at time management skills

❖ To formulate your overall "Game Plan for Life" in the areas of career, health, personal relations, attitude, finances, public service, education, and recreation

VOCABULARY

Positive Self-Direction	*Happiness*
Success	*Losers*
Winners	*Goal*
Winning	*Winning Self-Direction*

The secret of **Positive Self-Direction** is establishing a clearly defined goal and then acting on it. Most people spend more time planning a party, studying the newspaper, or making a holiday gift list, than they do in planning their lives. Winners set their daily goals the afternoon or evening before. They list on paper in a priority sequence at least six major things to do tomorrow. When they start in the morning, they go down the list checking off the items they have accomplished, adding new ones and carrying over onto the next day's itinerary those they did not complete.

Can you imagine if you did your grocery shopping without a list? What if you just went down to the supermarket to see what was going on, to sort of play it by ear and find yourself? You'd see all the television-advertised displays, a potpourri of irresistible goodies and items: Teenage Mutant Ninja Turtles Cereal, new improved Twinkies, Batman decals, the new Mister Clean, White Tornadoes (with special foaming action), Bionic Puppy Chow, two-second microwave TV dinners, and Waterless Dishwasher Soap. You'd be overwhelmed by items you didn't know about, didn't need, and didn't really want. Here you went to the supermarket for lettuce, tomatoes, and the ingredients for a nice salad, but since you didn't write it down and didn't really have it defined, you came home with things you didn't want.

Since the mind is a specific biocomputer, it needs specific instructions and directions. The reason most people never reach their goals is that they don't define them, learn about them, or ever seriously consider them as believable or achievable. In other words, they never set their goals. Winners can tell you where they are going, what they plan to do along the way, and who will be sharing the adventure with them.

Setting Goals

Winners in life – that one in one hundred people – are set apart from the rest of humanity by one of their most important developed traits – *Positive Self-Direction*. They have a game plan for life. Every winner knows where he or she is going day by day – every day.

Winners are goal and role oriented. They set goals and get what they want – consistently. They are self-directed on the road to fulfillment. Fulfillment or **success** has been defined as the progressive realization of goals that are worthy of the individual.

Winner's Edge

Who Are the Winners?

Winners, in my opinion, are those individuals who in a very natural, free-flowing way, seem to consistently get what they want from life. They put themselves together across the board – in their personal, professional, and community lives. They set and achieve goals that benefit others as well as themselves. You don't have to get lucky to win at life, nor do you have to knock other people down or gain at the expense of others. **Winning** is taking the talent or potential you were born with, and have since developed, and using it fully toward a purpose that makes you feel worthwhile according to your own internal standards. **Happiness**, that state of well-being and content-ment, is the natural by-product of living a worthwhile life. It is not a goal to be chased after or sought.

Happiness is the natural experience of winning your own self-respect, as well as the respect of others. Happiness should not be confused with indulgence, escapism, or hedonistic pleasure-seeking. You can't drink, inhale, or snort happiness. You can't buy it, wear it, drive it, swallow it, inject it, or travel to it! Happiness is the journey, not the destination. The "human" system is goal-seeking by design and, using a very basic analogy, may be compared to a homing torpedo system or an automatic pilot. Set your target and this self-activated system, constantly monitoring feedback signals from the target area and adjusting the course setting in its own navigational guidance com-puter, makes every correction necessary to stay on target and score a hit. Programmed incompletely, nonspecifically, or aimed at a target too far out of range, the "homing torpedo" will wander erratically around until its propulsion system fails or it self-destructs.

And so it is with each individual "human system" in life. Set a goal and this self-motivated system adjusts the self-image settings in its subconscious robot achievement mechanism to make every decision necessary to reach the goal. Programmed with vague random thoughts, or fixed on an unrealistic goal too far out of sight, the "human system" will wander aimlessly around its world until it wears itself out, or until it self-destructs.

Winners are people with a definite purpose in life. **Losers** are people who wander aimlessly through life or self-destruct. No one has given more clarity to the "human necessity for purpose" than Dr. Viktor Frankl, visiting scholar at the United States International University in San Diego, California. A psychiatrist in Vienna at the outbreak of World War II, Frankl was a prisoner in Nazi concentration camps for the duration of the war. Frankl arrived at his conclusions about *Man's Search for Meaning* (the title of his classic book on the subject), experiencing three years of horror in such death camps as Auschwitz and Dachau.

Observing himself and his comrades stripped of literally everything – families, professions, possessions, clothing, health, and dignity, he gradually developed his concepts concerning human purpose. Narrowly escaping the gas chambers and death by brutality many times, Frankl studied the behavior of both captors and captives with a curious detachment, and lived to put his observations in writing. We in America have been reminded of the impact of this human suffering in timeless motion picture and television dramatizations such as the *Holocaust*.

Perhaps more than any other authority on human behavior, Frankl's knowledge is first-hand and springs from objective evaluations of destitute humans living with the daily probability of death. These experiences enabled him to make a sharp departure from the theories of Sigmund Freud. For example, Freud taught that individuals differed in outlook and attitude while healthy, but that if humans were deprived of food, their behavior would become more and more uniform as they resorted to the level of their basic "animal-like" instincts. But Frankl states, "In the concentration camps we witnessed to the contrary; we saw how, faced with the identical situation, one man degenerated while another attained virtual saintliness."

He noticed that men and women were able to survive the trials of starvation and torture when they had a purpose for their existence. Those who had no reason for staying alive died quickly and easily. The ones who lived through Auschwitz (*about one in twenty*) were almost without exception individuals who had made themselves accountable to life – there was something they wanted to do or a loved one they wanted to see.

In the death camps, inmates told Frankl that they no longer expected anything from life. He would point out to them that they had it backward. "Life was expecting something of them. Life asks of every individual to discover what it should be." Purpose is an end to be obtained. The response to the challenges of life – purpose – is the healing balm that enables each of us to face up to adversity and strife.

Where there is life, there is hope.
Where there are hopes, there are dreams.
Where there are vivid dreams, repeated,
they become goals.

Developing Goals

What could an undernourished Black youth on the streets of San Francisco imagine, especially since he was suffering from a crippling disease associated with malnutrition called rickets, which made his legs weak and slightly bowed? He was given encouragement and leg braces. Not much of a head start in life. Yet this kid with the funny legs and the funny first name somehow developed a creative preview of coming attractions. When he was eleven years old, he attended a banquet honoring the legendary National Football League running back, Jim Brown. "I'll break every record you set," the youngster promised Brown. This kid has since shortened his funny first name, because his name is seen and used so much today. You may not remember little Orenthal, but you certainly do recognize the great O. J. Simpson, who set rushing records and is now a well-known TV sports commentator and product spokesperson.

A **goal** is the desired outcome toward which all effort is directed. Goals become the action plans and game plans that winners dwell on in intricate detail – knowing that achievement is almost automatic when the goal becomes an inner commitment. *What kind of goals are you committed to?* For many people – the thousands of Losers in daily life – getting through the day is their goal and as a result, they generate just enough energy and initiative to do that. Their goal is to watch television – soap operas by day and situation comedies by night. Having no goals of their own, they sit in a semi-stupor night after night with tunnel vision and watch TV actors and actresses enjoying themselves, earning money, and pursuing their careers and their goals.

Since we become what we think of most of the time, whatever we are thinking of now, we are unconsciously moving toward the achievement of that thought. For an alcoholic, this could be the next drink – for a drug addict, the next fix – for a surfer, the next wave. Divorce, bankruptcy, illness are all goals spawned out of negative attitudes and habit patterns. There have been studies conducted by the insurance industry concerning retired military officers and businessmen who were looking forward to retiring and just doing nothing after 30 years of hard work. Do you know that they live an average of four to seven years in retirement? Not much time to enjoy their pensions and just do nothing!

We all have the potential and the opportunity for success in our lives. It takes just as much energy and effort for a bad life as it does for a good life. And yet, millions of us lead unhappy, aimless lives – existing from day to day, year to year, confused, frustrated, in a prison of our own making. **Losers** are people who have never made the decision that could set them free. They have not decided what to do with their lives, even in our free society. They go to work to see what happens and you know what happens – they spend all their time making someone else's goals come true.

About 95 percent of humans can be compared to ships without rudders. Subject to every shift of wind and tide, they're helplessly adrift. And while they fondly hope that they'll one day drift into a rich and successful port, they usually end up on the rocks and run aground. But those five per cent who win, who have taken the time and exercised the discipline to decide on a destination and to chart a course, sail straight and far, reaching one port after another, and accomplishing more in just a few years than the rest accomplish in a lifetime. Every sea captain knows his next port of call, and even though he cannot see his actual destination for fully 99 percent of his voyage, he knows what it is, where it is and that, barring an unforeseen catastrophe, he'll surely reach it if he keeps doing certain things a certain way each day.

Winners in life start with lifetime goals. What do I stand for? What would I defend to the end? What would I want people to say about

Lifetime Goals

me after I am gone? Winners know how important time-priority goals are. A five-year plan. A one-year program. A six-month campaign. A summer project. But most of all, Winners know that the most important time frames are the groups of minutes in every day. Most people waste most of their waking hours every day going through the motions, chatting idly, shuffling papers, putting off decisions, reacting, majoring in minors, and concentrating on trivia. They spend their time in low priority tension-relieving, rather than high priority goal-achieving activities. Since they fail to plan, they are planning to fail by default.

Winning Self-Direction is setting goals that are realistic and meaningful to you. They should be specific. The mind, which operates like a homing torpedo or automatic pilot, is a robot computer – it gets what you set. It can't function properly without specific data. It can't relate to nebulous, vague, or general terms like "happiness," "wealth," or "health." It does respond to $3,000 a month, a new car, a desired weight of 175 for a man or 120 pounds for a woman, and blood pressure of 118 over 88.

The secret of *Positive Self-Direction* is in establishing a clearly defined goal, writing it down, and then dwelling on it morning and night, with words, pictures, and emotions as if you had already achieved it. For each of your goals, assemble support material, news articles, books, tapes, pictures cut out of magazines, consumer reports, cost estimates, color swatches, samples, etc. Review these often.

Review your goals with Winners and experts who have proven records of success in actually accomplishing what you have set out to do. Differentiate between those who want to sell you and those who are sincere in wanting to help you. One of the best ways is to pay someone strictly for advice and counsel, someone with no end product or other service to sell.

We do become what we think about most. And no wind blows in favor of a ship without a destination. The person without a purpose is like a ship without a rudder.

One ship sails East, another West,
by the selfsame winds that blow.
'Tis the set of the sail and not the gale,
that determines the way they go.
Like the winds of the sea
are the ways of time,
as we voyage along through life.
'Tis the set of the soul that determines the goal,
And not the calm or the strife.

Get behind the helm. Plan the work and work the plan. A day at a time. Decide now on your goals. Force your goals into your subconscious with unrelenting practice – daily rehearsal. See yourself achieving them one by one. Make winning your game plan in life. *And Win today!*

REVIEW

Read this Positive Self-Direction Review several times over the period of one month to etch it in your memory.

Winners in life have clearly defined game plans and purposes. They know where they're going every day, every month, every year. Their objectives range all the way from daily priorities to lifetime goals. And when they're not actively pursuing their goals, they're thinking about them – hard! They know the difference between goal-achieving acts and those which are merely tension-relieving . . . and they concentrate on the former. *Winners* say, "I have a plan to make it happen. I'll do what's necessary to get what I want." *Losers* say, "I'll try to hang in there – muddle through the day somehow."

Purpose is the engine that powers our lives. Everyone has purpose. For some it is to eat, for others it is to get through the day, and for others it is revenge or getting even. For *Winners* – personal growth, contribution, creative expression, and sharing, loving relationships seem to be common goals that make them such uncommon people. Clearly defined, written goals are the tools which make purpose achievable. Since the mind is a specific biocomputer it needs specific instructions and directions. The reason most people never reach their goals is that they don't define them, learn about them, or ever seriously consider them as believable or achievable. In other words, they never set them. They fail by default. *Winners* can tell you where they are going, approximately how long it will take, why they are going, what they plan to do along the way, and who will be sharing the adventure with them. Get a game plan for life!

Thought-Provoking Questions

1. Why is 1% of humanity different? What makes them different?

2. What does the quotation, "Happiness is the journey, not the destination" mean? What do we have to do to make ourselves happy before we get there?

3. What determines a person's quantity *(years)* and quality of life?

4. What are the qualities of a Winner based on *Positive Self-Direction*?

    What are the characteristics of a Loser based on *Positive Self-Direction*?

5. What do you need to formulate your "Game Plan for Life"?

6. Imagine yourself in your later years of life. You overhear your grandchildren telling their friends about your life and your accomplishments. What would you like them to say about you?

Strategies for Achieving Self-Direction

1. What are your lifetime goals?
    What do you want people to say about you?
    How do you want to be remembered?

2. What are your time-priority goals in the next five years? *Write one major goal in each of the eight areas:*

    ❖ *Career* _____

    ❖ *Health* _____

    ❖ *Personal Relations* _____

❖ *Attitude* _____

❖ *Finances* _____

❖ *Public Service* _____

❖ *Education* _____

❖ *Recreation* _____

3. List your top priority goals for the *next year* using the eight categories as above.

❖ *Career* _____

❖ *Health* _____

❖ *Personal Relations* _____

❖ *Attitude* _____

❖ *Finances* _____

❖ *Public Service* _____

❖ *Education* _____

❖ *Recreation* _____

4. Monthly Goals

What will you do?

Where will you go?

With whom will you communicate?

5. Set weekly and daily goals. What do you need or want to accomplish today? Tomorrow? The next day?

6. What is your most important lifetime career goal?

7. What will you be doing professionally in five years?

8. What can you do to move toward that five-year professional goal?

9. What is your most important one-year professional goal?

10. What will you do to reach that one-year goal?

11. What is your most important priority for the next month? For next week? For today?

12. What will you do to get the goals accomplished?

Self-Direction Action Reminders

For best results in goal achieving, use these basic rules.

Set short-range goals (*day, week, month, six months*)

Set lower-level goals (*relatively easy to accomplish*)

Set incremental goals (*little by little, part of the big objective*)

Get group reinforcement (*regularly consult a support group interested in the same achievement*)

Ceremonialize the achievement (*certificate, reward, dinner, trip, recreation, new clothing, etc.*)

2

POSITIVE SELF-IMAGE

*What you think you see
is what you get*

*Your self-image
is either your
life handicap
or your
autopilot for Winning*

AIMS

❖ To develop and focus on your own *Positive Self-Image*

❖ To explore ways to change or improve your self-image through the key factor known as imagination

❖ To differentiate between the roles your conscious and sub-conscious minds play with regard to self-image

❖ To identify and practice the requirements for any permanent change in personality

VOCABULARY

Self-Image	*Conscious Mind*
Positive Self-Image	*Judge*
Imagination	*Robot*
Life-Controlling Mechanism	*Imagineering*
Subconscious Mind	*Winner's Circle*

Individuals behave, not in accordance with reality, but in accordance with their perception of reality. How the individual feels about himself or herself is everything, for all that he or she ever does or aspires to do will be predicated on that all-important concept which is **self-image**, or "concept of self." **Positive Self-Image** is taking that self-concept and empowering it to make you the person you want to be.

Self-Image

Whether we realize it or not, each of us has in our mind a videotape cassette, a very complicated videocassette containing *(by the time we're 30 years old)* some three trillion pictures of ourselves. This videotape may be vague and ill-defined to our conscious awareness. In fact, it may not be consciously recognizable at all. But it is there, complete to the last detail. This self-image is our own conception of the "sort of person I am." It has been built by our own beliefs about ourselves.

Most of these beliefs about ourselves have unconsciously been formed from our past experiences, our successes and failures, our humiliations, our triumphs, and the way other people have reacted to us, especially in early childhood. From all these we mentally construct a "self," or a "videotape of a self." Once an idea or belief about ourselves goes into this picture, it becomes true as far as we, personally, are concerned. We do not question its validity, but proceed to act upon it just as if it were true.

Each of us, from childhood on, weaves our own intricate web of self-images out of notions, out of comments from our parents, and environmental training from our teachers and friends. First as offhand notions, like flimsy cobwebs, then with practice, they become cables to strengthen or shackle our lives. Children's self-images are very pliable and susceptible to external guidance and criticism. Young students who are treated as though they are mentally slow by teachers and parents will assume that they are, indeed, inferior to normal children. *It is not what you "are" that holds you back, it's "what you think you are not."*

A young primary grade school teacher conducted an experiment with her pupils. With approval from their parents, she told her class that

Are Blue Eyes Brighter?

"recent scientific reports had verified that children with blue eyes have greater natural learning abilities than children with brown eyes." She had them make up little signs designating them as "Blue Eyes" or "Brown Eyes" which were hung around their necks. After a week or so, the achievement level of the "Brown Eyes" group fell measurably, while the performance of the "Blue Eyes" improved significantly. She then made a startling announcement to the class. She had made a mistake! It was the "blue or lighter eyes" who were the "weaker" students and the "brown or dark eyes" who were the "stronger" students. Up went the image and achievement of the "Brown Eyes." Down, down came the performance of the "Blue Eyes." Talk about the power of suggestion!

The student who sees him or herself as an "F" student will invariably find that his or her report card bears that out. The report card is "proof." A young girl or boy who has an image of her or himself as the sort of person nobody likes will find indeed that she or he is avoided at the school dance. Such thinking literally invites rejection. Self-conscious expression, overanxiousness to please, or perhaps unconscious hostility toward those who may affront, all act to drive away those whom the student would attract. Each of us, from childhood, weaves our own intricate web of self-images out of the beliefs born in response to every thought and experience, every humiliation and triumph – every loss and win.

Just as with "stronger" and "weaker" students there is the image of the "stronger" and "weaker" sex. The male versus female syndrome. The woman's role in society used to be dominantly shaped by a restricted self-image as a result of associations with the "weaker sex" or "lower," "slower," and "lesser" potentials. The emergence of women as individuals in society has been a major sociological movement in this century. As the self-image of women is elevated, up goes behavior and achievement, down come the self-imposed and outer-imposed barriers and out come new opportunities for expression. Though this may seem an oversimplification, in the beginning we need to oversimplify things in order to understand them.

Each of us, male or female, has developed a self-image concerning every talent, every characteristic, and every performance. "I'm a lousy cook – I can't boil an egg." "I'm a good dancer." "I have a great sense of humor." "I have a terrible memory." "I'm a sensitive, warm person." "I'm never on time." "I'm a true Leo." "I'm a born Loser." Each of us is controlled by these "mental pictures" we have formed. We cannot outgrow these limits we place on ourselves – we can only set new limits within which we must live.

All Winners develop and actively think about *Positive Self-Image*. Winners act like Winners – imagining with pictures, feelings, and words the roles they want to play. They give themselves a preview of coming attractions. *What you "see" is what you get. Who you "feel" is who you are.*

Imagination Rules Our World

You are a unique gift of creation. And what you do with yourself is almost entirely based upon your imagination of your possibilities. Every living organism has a built-in guidance system to help it achieve its goal, which is, in very general terms, to live. In the more primary forms, the goal to live simply means physical survival for both the individual and the species. The built-in mechanism or instinct in animals is limited to finding food and shelter, avoiding or overcoming enemies, and procreation to ensure the survival of the species. In the human being, the goal to live means much more than mere survival. Humans have certain emotional and spiritual needs, which animals do not have.

We often overlook the fact that human beings have a success instinct much more marvelous and much more complex than that of any animal. Animals cannot select their goals; their goals are preset. Their success mechanism is limited to those inborn, goal images which are called instincts. The success instinct in the human being, however, has something that animals will never possess, and this is **imagination**. That imagination has the power to create mental images of things not present in reality. Thus, the human being of all creatures is more than a creature. He or she is also a creator. The human being is the only creature on the earth that can direct his or her success mechanism by the use of the creative imagination, or imagining ability. Napoleon said, *"Imagination rules the world."* Einstein put it more simply: *"Imagi-*

nation is the world." The way you picture your world, the way you perceive it, is the world in which you live.

The imagination we hold of ourselves, or our self-image, determines the kind and scope of person we are – it is our **Life-Controlling Mechanism.** Our self-image dwells at the subconscious level of thinking. The **subconscious mind** controls mental activities just below the threshold of consciousness. The **conscious mind** is the upper level of mental thought, characterized by sensation, emotion, and volition. The conscious level of thinking, responsible for collecting information from the environment, storing it in memory, and making rational decisions, can be compared to a judge. The subconscious level of thinking, responsible for autonomic body control such as breathing and heart-beat and goal-seeking can be compared to a robot.

Self-Image on Automatic Pilot

Guidance computers are devices which can be programmed to seek a target. They are installed in projectiles like the torpedo and the ballistic missile which are then guided by these highly sophisticated electronic systems that seek the target unerringly through the use of electronic data feedback. The human brain operates similarly but is far more marvelous and complex than any system man could ever invent.

With the homing torpedo, you set a target and its self-activated system, constantly monitoring feedback signals from the target area and adjusting the course setting in its own navigational guidance computer, makes every correction necessary to stay on target and score a hit. Programmed incompletely, nonspecifically, or aimed at a target too far out of range, the homing torpedo will wander erratically until its propulsion system fails or it self-destructs.

Set a personal goal or create an image and this self-motivated system, constantly monitoring self-talk and environmental feedback about the goal, adjusts the self-image settings in its subconscious creative achievement mechanism to make every decision necessary to reach the goal.

For further illustration, let's call the conscious level of thinking the **"Judge,"** and the subconscious level of thinking the **"Robot."** The first important point in the relationship of these two elements is that the Judge cannot make a decision until clearing it with the Robot or subconscious. The Robot checks its memory bank, which houses the all-important self-image and instantaneously relays available data back to the Judge for action.

It would seem natural that your Judge would control your Robot – in a master/slave type relationship. Incredibly, the reverse is true! The subconscious Robot controls the conscious Judge level of thinking. Action frequently takes place without consultation with the Judge, but no action ever takes place without reference to the Robot. Information fed into your Robot's memory bank stays there. The billions of separate items of input over a lifetime are all there awaiting retrieval. They can never be willfully erased by you. They can be overridden or modified, but you're stuck with them for life.

For example, brain surgery by world authority Dr. Wilder Penfield at the Montreal Neurological Institute strongly supports this premise – literally confirms it as a fact. In their research, when brain cells were stimulated with an electrode, patients reported the sensation of re-living scenes from the past. The recall was so vivid that all details were present, including sounds, colors, and odors. Not just remembering, but reliving the experiences!

During every moment of our lives we program our Robot to work for us or against us. Since it is only a mechanism, having no judging function, it strives to meet the objectives and goals we set for it, regardless of whether they are positive or negative, true or false, right or wrong, safe or dangerous. Its sole function is to follow instructions implicitly, based upon previous input, like a computer reading it tape and responding automatically.

Scientists agree that the human nervous system cannot tell the difference between an actual experience and an experience imagined vividly, emotionally, and in detail. This is why *attitude determines success.* Because attitude is an imagined inclination toward the achievement of a certain event. Therefore, attitude is everything, since the human system cannot tell the difference between an actual performed experience and an imagined synthetic experience.

Many of your everyday decisions are based upon information about yourself which has been stored as "truth" – but is just a figment of your own imagination shaded by your environment. You are a slave to your subconscious Robot, which houses your all-important self-image. If you try to make a change in yourself at the conscious Judge level by using will power, the change usually will be only temporary.

Let us assume you have been a one-pack-a-day smoker for ten years and decide to give it up by good old-fashioned, teeth-gritting will power. You go to the Judge and tell him or her you have given up smoking for good. The Judge wants to believe you, but is obligated to check all the evidence about your smoking record in the Robot's memory bank. The Robot checks the number of times you have tried to quit in the past and asks your self-image for a report. Your self-image has witnessed you as a smoker for the past ten years and testifies that you still "see" yourself inside as a smoker. Back up comes the Robot's report automatically, almost instantaneously, to the Judge. The Judge, who makes rational, conscious decisions based on testimony, has no alternative but to find you "guilty" of being a "smoker" who is likely to break his or her promise one day soon.

Whenever your Judge and Robot come in conflict, the Robot has the best chance of winning unless newly acquired fears or desires are strong enough to override it. *Any permanent change in your personality or behavior should first involve a change in your self-image, reinforced by a change in lifestyle. Then your long-range behavior or performance will follow.* Your behavior, personality, or achievement level is usually consistent with your self-image.

Winner's Circle

Do you view your self-image as your life "handicap" or your "achievement mechanism?" Are you a lifetime slave to your Robot? You can't escape from your self-image! Oh, you can turn to alcohol, drugs, or mental depression. Losers take this trip every day! You can even get amnesia and forget the whole thing. Winners control their self-image and change it as they desire. They elevate their self-image and enlarge their universe. Winners understand the tenacity of a time-grown self-image and realize that it takes days and weeks of constant **"imagineering"** (*taking ideas and developing them into reality*) and simulation to modify or put new inputs on top of the old programs. It requires self-discipline, persistence, and dedication to change your image totally from the inside.

Winners know that worry, anxiety, hostility, and depression are negative, destructive users of their creative imaginations. Winners dwell on and hold the self-image of that person they would most like to become. They get a vivid, clear, emotional, sensory picture of themselves as if they had already achieved their goal.

Winners tell themselves over and over again with words, pictures, concepts, and emotions that they are winning each important personal victory now. Winners practice on and off their playing field of life. They create in their **imagination** or simulate each experience they want. Every winner I've ever met in every walk of life, male or female, uses the technique of mental simulation every day to modify his or her own self-image. I met a world champion Russian figure skater and she said, "I rarely fall because I practice each sequence in my imagination at night with my eyes closed and could successfully perform my routine blindfolded with no hesitation."

"One small step for man, one giant leap for mankind." These words were spoken by Neil Armstrong, whose vision began as a young boy. In an interview immediately following his historic first step on the moon, he said, *"Ever since I was a little boy, I dreamed I would do something important in aviation."* It is fascinating that the dreams, daydreams, and imagination of a child can shape a destiny so dramatically that this particular youth was to grow up to make the most significant footprints on the sands of time of any aviator during the first century of man's flight.

Like children playing "Let's Pretend," Winners play the role of whomever they want to be. They know their little Robots can't tell the difference between "the real me" and "the one I see." They see themselves standing in the **Winner's Circle**, that area where people with *Positive Self-Image* mentally visualize themselves attaining the goals they've set. They feel that solid weight of the gold medal around their necks. They hear the approval of the crowd. They smell the roses in the Rose Bowl. They touch the diploma in their hand. They feel the self-esteem of their personal achievement, however lofty or humble, in advance. *Winners feel like Winners. Winners "see" through the eyes of Winners.*

What do you "see" for you today? Who will you be tomorrow? *Think Win!*

REVIEW

Read this Positive Self-Image Review several times over the period of one month to etch it in your memory.

Winners are especially aware of the tremendous importance of their self-image – and of the role their imagination can play in the creation and upgrading of the self-image. They know the self-image acts as a subconscious life-governing device – that if in your self-image you can't possibly see yourself doing something, achieving something, you literally cannot do it! They also know the self-image can be changed since the subconscious is incapable of differentiating between a real success and a success *imagined* again and again vividly and in full detail. A *Winner*'s Self-Talk is "I see myself changing, growing, achieving, winning!" *Losers* say, "They're *my* problems, faults, and stupidities . . . and I'm stuck with 'em."

Your behavior and performance usually are consistent with your self-image. Your self-image is an intricately woven concept made up of all your feelings, fears and emotional responses to each and every personal experience up to the present. As with any learned activity or skill, the self-image is housed at the subconscious or automatic level of thinking. What you perceive as real is filtered or shaded differently from what others perceive by your time-grown, robot-like self-image. What you imagine as being real, with frequency, becomes your version of reality. *Winners* imagine and fantasize that person they would most like to become – and the robot self-image reads the script, memorizes it, and acts accordingly.

Thought-Provoking Questions

1. Discuss the following: "It's not what you 'are' that holds you back, it's 'what you think you are not.'"

2. Each of us, from childhood, weaves our own intricate web of self-images out of beliefs born in response to every thought and experience, every humiliation and triumph, every loss and win. How can we shape and determine our future self-image?

3. Recalling the experiments identifying blue and then brown-eyed children as stronger students, when has your self-image faltered due to outside influences? What did you do or what could you have done to overcome the negative stigmatism?

4. How could you develop a more *Positive Self-Image* using your conscious and subconscious mind?

5. What is the basis for many of our everyday decisions? How does this affect our self-image?

6. How can creative imagination (visualization) help to improve your self-image?

Strategies for Achieving Positive Self-Image

1. Go for a walk on the beach or in the country or park and recall your childhood play:

   ❖ Dust off and "oil" your imagination. It rules your world.

2. Set aside time during the day or evening. As you relax during this time, imagine yourself achieving and enjoying your most dreamed of personal desires. Do this as though you were previewing the following three television shorts:

❖ *Picture one sequence achieving a professional triumph. Imagine the award ceremony, promotion announcement, or raise in pay.*

❖ *Picture another scene involving family happiness. Imagine a special reunion or an outing together.*

❖ *Picture another setting in which you alone are relishing a personal victory. Imagine a sports championship, weigh-in at a health club.*

Get the actual sensation of each event and how good it feels to experience each one.

3. Read a biography or autobiography this month and each month:

   ❖ The life story of someone who has reached the top in your profession, in your major hobby or sport, or just someone you admire.

   ❖ As you read, imagine yourself achieving the same accomplishments as the person about whom you are reading.

4. Write a two-page resume of your professional and personal assets as if you were going to apply for the job of a lifetime.

   ❖ Instead of past experience, list your maximum current potential and ultimate future potential.

   ❖ Read this autobiography every week, revise it every two months.

   ❖ Show it only to those individuals whom you believe can and will help your toward your goals.

5. Since the self-image is the conceptual, visual display of self-esteem, you may wish to take a look at your surroundings and analyze how they represent you.

❖ Take stock this weekend of those images with which you display yourself: *clothes, auto, home, garage, closet, dresser drawers, desk, photos, lawn, garden, etc.*

Are they cluttered with old junk? Are they neatly organized? Are you happy with their appearances?

Make a priority list to get rid of all clutter and sharpen up all the expressions of your life.

3

POSITIVE SELF-DISCIPLINE

Habits begin as harmless thoughts
- like flimsy cobwebs -
then, with practice,
become unbreakable cables
to shackle or strengthen our lives

I Can
is energizing
Say it to yourself
right now: I Can

AIMS

❖ To list the influences that form and develop your habits

❖ To utilize a formula for learning a skill, changing a habit, developing a goal, or improving self-image

❖ To apply the use of mental simulation used by *Winners* in formulating goals, changing habits, or improving self-image

❖ To form or break at least one habit

❖ To discuss the advantages and uses of *Positive Self-Discipline*

❖ To master the three components of *Positive Self-Discipline*

VOCABULARY

Habit	*Repetition*
Desire	*Simulation*
Positive Self-Discipline	*Positive Self-Talk*

A **habit** is a behavior pattern that has been acquired through frequent repetition. This mode of behavior can become so imprinted upon our subconscious that the patterns become completely involuntary. Habits start out as off-hand remarks, magazine advertisements, friendly hints, experiments – like flimsy cobwebs with little substance. They grow with practice, layer upon layer – thought upon thought – fused with imagination and emotion until they become like steel cables – unbreakable. Habits are attitudes which develop and come to control your everyday life. We spend our most of our time practicing our bad habits rather than our good ones or even looking for good ones.

Desire is a powerful motivating emotion which attracts, opens, directs, and encourages plans and goals. You may be self-motivated by desire. You may feel you are in control. You may expect to go to the moon. You may imagine yourself on the moon. But you will never even get near the launching pad without persistent self-discipline. Up to now, it all seemed so simple. You tell your "robot subconscious achievement mechanism" that you want a new self-image and assume it will happen.

Well, there's a little more effort involved. You have been the way you are for some time now. And every day, your actions and reactions usually confirm and support your present self-image. You constantly talk to yourself every minute you are awake maintaining and justifying who you are today. This has gone on for years. Your Robot has matured into a control room full of some very well-established habits!

Habits

Positive Self-Discipline is the mental practice from within to make or break habits, change self-image, or achieve goals. Many people define self-discipline as "doing without." A better definition for discipline is "doing within." Self-discipline is the commitment to memory of those thoughts and emotions that will override current information stored in the subconscious memory bank. Through relentless **repetition**, the technique of practicing over and over through self-talk or imagination, the penetration of these new inputs into our subconscious results in the creation of a new or changed habit, self-image, or goal.

Positive Self- Discipline

Most people forget the simple routine for learning a skill or habit: *Desire, Information, Simulation,* and *Repetition.* Desire says, "I Want," "I Can," "I See Opportunity," and "I Will." Desire looks to the future and is a strong, positive magnet. Self-discipline is gathering the information necessary to develop and pursue your goals, change your habits, or improve your self-image.

All the Winners I've ever met in every walk of life, male or female, use the technique of mental simulation every day in their imagination. They try to visualize each experience they want, goal they desire to reach, or habit they wish to change, and absorb it into their subconscious. This process imprints their desired result on the brain. Self-discipline is repetition – telling yourself over and over with words, pictures, concepts, and emotions that you are winning each important personal victory now. Winners practice constantly, on and off the playing field, in and out of school or their career.

Winners Simulate Winning

Astronauts are masters at mental **simulation** *(creating and practicing experiences in your mind).* They practice bobbing up and down in a rubber raft at sea, responding to the feeling of "weightlessness" to be experienced in outer space. They practice on the desert with a Simulated Lunar Excursion Module, as if they were landing it on the surface of the moon. Hour after hour, month after month, they visualize, memorize, and imitate the exact steps that NASA scientists have imagined would take them safely to the moon and back.

When Neil Armstrong took the first step on the moon and transmitted his reactions back to Mission Control in Houston, he commented, "It was beautiful, just like our drills." On a later moon expedition, Apollo Captain Conrad commented, "It's just like old home week. I feel like I've been here many times before. After all, we have been rehearsing this moment for the past four years!"

French skier Jean-Claude Killy won the giant slalom in his imagination first. He used mental simulation to practice skiing and gain confidence. Feet together, weight properly balanced, correct knee position, down the fall line, watch for moguls, feel the pure, crisp snow, the wind, the speed, the exhilaration of doing it all yourself. For champions, it's the *Winning Edge*. For beginners, a great way to conquer fear. After all, in your imagination, you never fall!

Reader's Digest some years ago told of a class of high school basketball players with similar skills who were divided into three separate groups to conduct an experiment. Group I was told not to practice shooting free throws for one month. Group II was told to practice shooting free throws in the gym every afternoon for one hour for one month. Group III was told to practice shooting free throws in their imagination every afternoon for one hour for one month. Group I, with no practice for a month, slipped from a 39 percent to a 37 percent free throw average. Group II, who practiced in the gym, increased from a 39 to a 41 percent average. *The players in Group III, who practiced in their imaginations, went from a 39 to a 42.5 percent average!*

Ridiculous. How could your free throw average improve more from practicing in your imagination than from actual practice with the ball and basket in the gym? Simply because in your imagination you never miss! Another basket and another – practice makes perfect. In the gym, when you make three in a row, your self-talk might be, "I hope I can continue" or "I wonder when I'll miss" or "That was a lucky one." In the gym, when you miss one or two, your self-talk might be, "Get it in, you klutz!" or "There I go again."

Your **Positive Self-Talk** *(mental dialogue with yourself to effect positive results)* after a performance usually conforms to your current self-image and keeps your aim locked near your present performance. Self-discipline through concentrated self-talk is needed even when a sudden, dramatic physical change takes place outwardly deserving of a new self-image.

Dr. Maxwell Maltz, plastic surgeon and author of *Psycho-Cybernetics*, found that after plastic surgery many individuals take about three weeks to become accustomed to their new faces. Gradually they begin to feel comfortable with their new "selves." Sometimes, however, the old self-image is so ingrained that even those who have been transformed from homely people to attractive ones have emotional difficulty in accepting the new self.

Dr. Maltz refers to one of his patients who had come to him with a pronounced, unattractive hook nose and who he altered to have a facial appearance not unlike a movie star's, with a perfectly shaped nose. Admiring the results in front of a mirror, Dr. Maltz happily queried, "How do you like the new, beautiful you?" She replied coldly, "I don't see much improvement. I still feel ugly!"

Another overt illustration of the power of the time-grown self-image is in the study of amputees. In reality – physically, consciously, and at the judgment level of thinking – the limb is gone. But, for several weeks, sometimes longer, the patient will experience pain, itching, or tingling in hands or feet that are no longer there. The image lingers on, long after the reality is changed!

If it requires several weeks to mentally accept a new self-image brought about by a permanent physical change – consider the self-discipline required to modify your behavior in order to change your habits or pursue your goals!

Winners Practice Positive Self-Discipline

History books and record books are full of Winners in life who have made it on their own by sheer determination and guts against all the odds. Winners are people who can do within while they are doing without. Helen Keller, O.J. Simpson, Eleanor Roosevelt, Mahatma Gandhi, Martin Luther King, and Albert Schweitzer all practiced self-discipline.

Examples of winning self-discipline have been seen in the experience of POWs returning from Viet Nam. They taught each other skills from rote memory, discussed and rediscussed boyhood experiences of mutual interest and value, created complete mental diaries while in solitary confinement, invented hundreds of money-making ideas and, perhaps most importantly, gained perspective by remembering and sharing ideals that are the foundation of their country's greatness.

Self-discipline in action! When Winners are in crisis, they work and practice to toughen themselves. They know that the imagination is the greatest tool in the universe! It *is* the universe to a prisoner of war.

Winners never quit. Winners never give up. Winners pick themselves up, dust themselves off, and do it all over again . . . better! Discipline yourself to win. Practice "within" when you are "without."

Control Your Self-Talk

Before every important performance in your life, whether it's taking a test, speaking in front of a group, communicating with employees, playing a sport, or dealing with loved ones – you should control your self-talk to elevate your best self-image of a winning performance. If you performed well, your self-talk should be "That's more like me." If you performed badly, your immediate self-talk should be "That's not like me, I perform better than that." Then you should replay the action correctly in your imagination.

Simulate Goals

Visualizing your desired goals or achievements can best be effected during relaxed times. This may be early in the morning upon awakening, during a walk or jog; commuting to work or school; or prior to sleeping.

Be Persistent

Be relentless in rehearsing your goal achievements. Both *Losing* and *Winning* are learned habits. It takes days and weeks of constant practice to overcome old entrenched attitudes and lifestyles. It does not happen overnight. *Make Winning your habit!*

Three Components of Self-Discipline

REVIEW

Read this Positive Self-Discipline Review several times over a period of one month to etch it in your memory.

Positive Self-Discipline is the ability to practice within. *Winners* are masters of the art of simulation. Like astronauts, championship athletes, great stage performers, skilled surgeons, and truly professional executives and salespeople, they practice flawless techniques in their minds over and over, again and again. They know that thought begets habit and they discipline their thoughts to create the habit of superb performance – the mark of a *Total Winner*. You may have desire. You may feel you are in control. You may expect to go to the moon. But you will never even get near the launching pad without persistent self-discipline.

Most people forget the simple routine for learning a skill or habit: *Desire, Information, Simulation,* and *Repetition.* We learned how to walk, drive, type, fly, speak a foreign language, ski, act in a play, etc. Why is it so difficult for us to apply learning to our most important life goals? Everything is habit-forming if it is repeated! Self-discipline alone can make or break a habit. Self-discipline alone can effect a permanent change in your self-image and in you. Self-discipline is the *Winning Edge* that achieves goals. Self-discipline is mental practice – the commitment to memory of those thoughts and emotions that will override current information stored in the subconscious memory bank. And through relentless repetition, the penetration of these new inputs into our "robot achievement mechanism" results in the creation of a new self-image.

A *Winner's* self-talk: "Of course I can do it! I've practiced it mentally a thousand times." *Losers* say "How can you expect me to do it? I don't know how!" Now you do! *Now you're a Winner!*

Thought-Provoking Questions

1. What is the simple routine for learning a skill or a habit? Why is it difficult to learn a new habit or skill?

2. Regarding *Positive Self-Discipline*, what makes Winners unique?

3. What is mental simulation? Where and when do you engage in it and for what purpose?

4. What skill or habit would you like to acquire?

5. Is it easier to establish or break a habit? What roles do the "Robot" and "Judge" play in this exercise of Self-Discipline?

6. What are the three components of *Positive Self-Discipline*? How can you use them to form or break a habit, establish a goal, or improve self-image?

Strategies for Developing Positive Self-Discipline

Positive Self-Discipline is the key to activating your new self-image, defined in the previous chapter. *Positive Self-Discipline* is simply practicing the ideas and skills you've been learning. It involves disciplining yourself to practice with relentless consistency. This practice forms positive habits, and habits, once formed, are automatic.

1. In the book *Psycho-Cybernetics*, Dr. Maxwell Maltz tells us it takes a minimum of three weeks to develop a habit. You have been given a scientifically proven, well-researched method for developing the positive habits of your choice. Are you willing to invest the time and energy necessary to develop new habits? Why or why not?

2. Which habits would you like to develop in the future? What habits have you formed which serve no useful purpose? Which habits have you formed that are harmful to you physically and mentally? How can you use *Positive Self-Talk* to eliminate these useless and harmful habits and replace them with positive, productive habits?

3. *Positive Self-Discipline* is an example of the universal law of cause and effect. In other words, before you can "reap the rewards," you must "pay the price." Are you willing to pay the price in effort and practice in order to accomplish what you want? Check your choice(s).

I will practice my simulations every day   _____

I'll practice almost every day   _____

I'll try to practice as often as I can   _____

I'm pretty busy and don't know when I'll practice   _____

You don't really believe this stuff works, do you?   _____

4. What will you need to discipline yourself to practice your simulations? What might be some roadblocks, obstacles, or excuses? What will you do to overcome these?

5. As a daily exercise, you should rehearse every important goal achievement simulation over and over in your imagination, as if you had already mastered that act.

6. Make a list of five necessary but unpleasant tasks that you have been putting off. Put a completion date after each task. Start and finish each task. Immediate action on unpleasant projects reduces stress and tension.

Task	Completion Date
1. _____	_____
2. _____	_____
3. _____	_____
4. _____	_____
5. _____	

7. Utilize one of the above tasks or select a new habit or skill to be incorporated in the following:

Desire: *I desire to* _____

Information: *I need to* _____

Simulation: *Use your imagination to* _____

Repetition: *Where* _____

                        When _____

                        Frequency _____

8. When you simulate and visualize your goals, envision the exact achievement of the specifics as if they had already been accomplished. For instance, see yourself at your desired weight or passing a final exam.

4

POSITIVE SELF-MOTIVATION

*Winners dwell on
their desires, not
their limitations*

Think of motivation as steam
Harness the steam to an engine,
and it can pull a thousand-ton train

AIMS

❖ To identify the differences between the terms *"Winners"* and *"Losers"* as they pertain to *Self-Motivation*

❖ To create a list of personal motives and benefits in relation to chosen goals

❖ To understand how the emotions of fear and desire affect motivation

❖ To explore limitations that inhibit motivation

❖ To identify and assess the effects of stress and anxiety on motivation

❖ To develop a *Positive Self-Talk* vocabulary

VOCABULARY

Motive

Motivation

Positive Self-Motivation

Fear

Positive Tension

Current Dominant Thought

The Winner's Edge

Motivation

Many people have the mistaken idea that personal motivation is an option – like an hors d'oeuvre which can be taken or left alone. But everything an individual does, whether positive or negative, intentional or unintentional, is the result of motivation. Everyone is self-motivated – a little or a lot – positively or negatively.

Motivation is a much maligned, overfranchised, overpromoted, and misunderstood term. The word **motive** is defined as an idea, need, emotion, or organic state which incites action. **Motivation** is a force which moves us to action, and it springs from inside the individual. Defined as a strong tendency toward or away from an object or situation, it can be learned and developed. It does not have to be inborn.

For too long, however, it has been wrongly assumed that motivation is extraneous – that it can be pumped in from the outside through incentives, pep talks, contests, rallies, and sermons. Such activities do provide concepts, encouragement, and inspiration for individuals to turn on their creative powers – but only if they want to. And that's the secret. Lasting change is effected only when the need for change is both understood and internalized. Until the reward or incentive has been interpreted and internalized, it has no motivating power.

Winners in life are people who have developed strong **Positive Self-Motivation**, the force that moves them in the direction of goals they have set. In the face of discouragement, mistakes, and setbacks, their inner drive keeps them moving upward toward self-fulfillment.

Fear and Desire

Motivation is an emotional state. The great physical and mental motivators in life – survival, hunger, thirst, revenge, love – are charged with emotion. Two key emotions dominate human motivation with opposite, but equally effective results – fear and desire. **Fear** is the most powerful negative motivator. It is the great compeller and the great inhibitor. Fear restricts, tightens, panics, forces, and ultimately scuttles plans and defeats goals. Desire, conversely, is like a strong, positive magnet. It attracts, opens, directs, and encourages plans and goals.

Fear and desire are poles apart, and lead to opposite destinies. Fear looks to the past – desire to the future! Fear vividly replays haunting experiences of failure, pain, disappointment, or unpleasantness, and is a dogged reminder that the same experiences are likely to repeat themselves. Desire triggers memories of pleasure and success and excites the need to replay these to create new winning experiences.

The consuming "prison" words of the fearful person are likely to be "I have to," "I can't," "I see risk," and "I wish." Desire says "I want to," "I can," "I see opportunity," and "I will." Desire is that emotional state between where you are and where you want to be. Winners have desire. They are dissatisfied with the status quo. They want change for the better. There never was a Winner who didn't want to Win. Desire is a magnetic, positive tension. Negative tension, induced by fear, creates stress, anxiety, sickness, and hostility; carried to extremes it can cause psychoses and death.

Positive Tension

Positive tension is an inner striving or unrest often manifested by a physiological indication of emotion. Positive tension, produced by desire, is like a bow pulled tautly to propel the arrow to the bullseye. Viktor Frankl, noted psychiatrist and founder of the psychotherapeutic school known as *"logotherapy,"* flatly stated that what a person actually needs is not a tensionless state, but the striving and struggling for a goal that is worthy of him or her. Winners respond positively to stress in life, just as professional athletes, executives, educators, doctors, and nurses respond successfully to stresses in their arenas.

Mike Nichols, Broadway director/producer, said, *"Nerves provide me with energy. They work for me. It's when I don't have them, when I feel at ease, that I get worried."* When you get "butterflies" in your stomach before a performance, accept them as butterflies. Butterflies are nice. When they start to eat you, they are like moths. Moths in your stomach are not nice. They cause ulcers.

One of the best-guarded secrets is the kind of self-motivation practiced by high achievers and effective leaders called **current dominant thought** that says since we always move in the direction of what we are thinking of most, it is imperative to concentrate our thoughts on the condition we want to achieve rather than try to move away from what we fear or don't want.

There are no limits other than self-imposed. The capacity of the human brain may be infinite. With this virtually untapped and limitless resource, why aren't we more creative, inventive, and successful? Laziness, to be sure, is one mental block. Why bother? Fear is another big block. It's too risky for me! And it isn't just fear of failure that holds us back. It's more often fear of success. Because we can't see our potential, we're beaten from the start, and so we make the excuse, "It's not worth it to succeed." But what we're really saying is, "I'm not worth the effort." This negative self-esteem, plus a low self-image resulting from negative attitudes, is the major energy gap preventing the release of full human actualization.

Winners Focus on Solutions

The mind cannot concentrate on the reverse of an idea. An excellent illustration of this statement is the true story concerning one of the world's most exciting World Series baseball games of the 1950s between the New York Yankees and the Milwaukee Braves. Warren Spahn, the great Milwaukee Hall of Famer, was on the mound for the Braves. Elston Howard, the power-hitting catcher for the Yankees, was batting at the plate. It was the classic confrontation – late innings, pitchers' duel, man on base, deciding game of the series. The tension was paramount.

The Milwaukee manager trotted out to the mound for a quick "motivation" conference with Spahn. "Don't give Howard a high, outside pitch – he'll knock it out of the park!" were the final words as the manager finished the pow-wow. Warren Spahn tried not to throw the ball high and outside. He tried to relax and aim low at the inside corner. Too late! Like a neon light the motivating image "high outside" was the dominant signal. It was a home run pitch.

After the game, which almost lost the series for the Braves (*thanks to Eddie Matthews, Milwaukee pulled it out*), Warren Spahn thought to himself, "I'll never again try to force my thought away from what I don't want, away from a feared result."

Perhaps as much as any superstar in sports and in business, Jack Nicklaus, the golfing legend, personifies the quality of *Positive Self-Motivation* by desire as opposed to fear. Nicklaus recently remarked, *"Imagine the mind to be a quart jar. I make sure the jar is always full of positive thoughts – intentions of hitting accurate, good shots."* The rest of us tend to fill the jar at least halfway with negative thoughts. We're thinking of what can go wrong with a shot, rather than what should go right. Nicklaus' mind is so permeated with the task at hand there's no room for negatives. He controls every move to a specific end under conditions where most of our minds would be going a hundred ways at once.

This tremendous ability to focus and concentrate on the currently dominant thought – on the winning action – is the mark of a winning superstar. Jack Nicklaus has applied this action quality to his many successful business enterprises. He has proven that when one concentrates on doing one thing extremely well, it will take seed and grow and multiply into many diversified opportunities. Winners know that their actions will be controlled by their current obsessions.

Risk as Opportunity

Winners see risk as opportunity. Winners see the rewards of success in advance. They do not fear the penalties of failure. The enervating powers of fear are unfortunate, for individuals so dominated cannot act with volition and positive intent; rather, they go through life reacting, defensive, and incapacitated. People who are dominated by stress are unable to change the world they live in – the world they live in alters them. It is a strange and sobering axiom that the thing we fear, we ourselves bring to pass.

Many years ago the English essayist James Allen wrote: *"They who have conquered doubt and fears have conquered failure. Their every thought is allied with power, and all difficulties are bravely met and wisely overcome."*

Desire is the perfect mental antidote for fear and despair. Desire sparks activity, which burns up excess adrenaline in the system, keeps the mind busy, and the hope of achievement alive. Inactivity breeds despondency, brings forth dark imaginings and distorts situations out of all proportion to reality. When fear begins to beg for attention, the Winner gets busy and things regain their proper perspective.

Norman Vincent Peale, an American clergyman who won fame for his writings like *The Power of Positive Thinking* (1952) and his radio and television programs, told the following story about Maurice Chevalier. For many decades Chevalier delighted audiences all over the world with his jaunty straw hat, crooning voice and whimsical smile. He was the debonair boulevardier, America's number one Frenchman.

Early during his brilliant career, Chevalier suffered a nervous breakdown just before he was to go on stage. He was ordered to rest in the southern part of France. "I'm a beaten man," he told the doctor. "I'm afraid of being a failure. There is no future for me now." He was advised to take long walks to repair his damaged nervous system. But the inner turmoil did not leave him. He was terribly afraid – he had lost all confidence.

After a time, when the doctor thought the actor was ready for it, he suggested that Chevalier entertain before a small group in the village hall. "But," said Maurice, "I am terrified at the thought. What guarantee is there that my mind will not go blank again, that the dizziness will not return?" "There is no guarantee, but you must not be afraid of failing. You are afraid to step on a stage again, and so you are telling yourself that you are finished. Fear is never a reason for quitting, it is only an excuse. When winning individuals encounter fear, they admit it and go on despite it. Don't be afraid to be afraid. Go on and perform even so."

Chevalier suffered untold agony of fear before his appearance in that little town in front of those people, but he went on and performed very well. Joy welled up inside him. "I knew that I had not permanently conquered fear. But I admitted it and went on despite it. The idea worked!"

After that evening, Maurice Chevalier performed before huge audiences everywhere. "There have been many moments of fear," said the entertainer. "The gentle doctor was right, there is no guarantee. But being frightened has never made me want to quit." Maurice added, "My own experience has taught me this. If you wait for the perfect moment when all is safe and assured, it may never arrive. Mountains will not be climbed, races won nor happiness achieved!"

And Maurice Chevalier achieved happiness. He never quit on life. He danced and sang his way into the hearts of millions for over eighty years. And his memory will linger, for he was a person who won over himself. He never settled for defeat. What have you settled for in life?

There is a disturbing philosophical movement today that associates drive and initiative solely with materialistic power and gain. While there does appear to be a growing obsession focused on the accumulation of nonessential personal possessions, this should not be confused with personal achievement and the pursuit of individual excellence. Disregarding all material rewards for high achievement, there is a pure personal pleasure which comes with achieving the difficult. The emotional spin-off that accompanies performance of the unusual or challenging personal test can range from a quiet flow of self-esteem to outright exhilaration, and is reason enough for the pursuit of excellence.

The Winner's Edge

After decades of quest, we now know that high achievers have a high degree of self-motivation. The enduring power that moves them to action comes from inside themselves. There seems to be only a fine line between the top five percent of the real achievers, the real Winners in society, and the rest of the pack. I call this fine line a demarcation, **The Winner's Edge**.

When I think of the *Winner's Edge*, I'm reminded of the difference between simple boiling water and powerful steam, which is used to power the giant steam catapults that are used to launch Navy jet aircraft from the flight deck of aircraft carriers. When water is heated to 211 degrees Fahrenheit, it is simply boiling water. However, when the temperature reaches 212 degrees, one degree higher, the water is converted into steam which is powerful enough to hurtle 60 tons of steel from a dead stop to 120 miles an hour in five seconds.

Scores of achieving people in every walk of life are all around us, yet few of us ever think of the long and arduous process that led them step-by-step to their goals. Who, for instance, remembers that Winston Churchill was a poor student, or that Althea Gibson came from the back alleys of Harlem to the front court at Wimbledon, that Franklin Delano Roosevelt had polio, that Beethoven was deaf, that Tom Dempsey kicked the longest field goal in NFL history with half a foot, or that Margaret Thatcher, the prime minister of England, lived over her father's grocery store in England until she was 21. They all wanted something special for themselves, in spite of their early track record. In spite of their bloodlines or their home lives, they all had the desire to win; they wanted to win and they expected to win.

Success is not reserved for the talented. It is not in a high I.Q. – not in the gifted birth – not in the best equipment – not even in ability. Success is almost totally dependent upon drive, focus, and persistence. The extra energy required to make an extra effort, to try another approach, to concentrate on the desired outcome, is the secret of winning. Out of desire comes the energy and will to win. *Get that urge to Win!*

REVIEW

Read this Positive Self-Motivation Review several times over the period of one month to etch it in your memory.

The *Positive Self-Motivation* of *Total Winners* derives from two sources: *1* their self-expectant personal and world view and *2* their awareness that, while fear and desire are among the greatest motivators, fear is destructive while desire leads to achievement, success, and happiness. With this in mind, they focus their thinking on the rewards of success and actively tune out fears of failure. *Losers* say: "I can't because. . ." *Winners* say "I want to . . ." and "I can!"

We are all self-motivated a little or a lot. Motivation is an inside job. Individuals are motivated by their fears, inhibitions, compulsions, and attractions. They are pushed away from or pulled toward concepts and people who act as negative or positive magnets. Realizing the almost impossible task of moving away from negative concepts such as "fat," "poor," and "sick". *Winners* focus on goals, desires, and solutions. Since most of our fears are based on dark imaginings, it is vital for us to dwell on our magnificent obsessions and desired results – to look at where we want to go, as opposed to that troubled place where we may have been or may still be hiding. People resist changing because it upsets their present security. People will change dramatically when it's a matter of life or death. *And people will change happily and effectively . . . when they want to.*

Thought-Provoking Questions

1. What are some physical and mental motivators in life?

2. What do you think affects a person's motivation level?

3. Why do people resist change?

4. How can "facing your fear" motivate you to reach or change your self-direction?

5. *For Discussion*
    Since we always move in the direction of what we are thinking of most, it is imperative to concentrate our thoughts on the condition we want to achieve rather than try to move away from what we fear or don't want.

6. *For Discussion*
    People who are dominated by stress are unable to change the world they live in. The world they live in alters them. Things we fear become our world.

Strategies for Achieving Self-Motivation

1. Replace the word "can't" with "can" in your daily vocabulary. "Can" applies to about 95 percent of the challenges you encounter.

2. Replace the word "try" with "will" in your daily vocabulary. This is a form of semantics and simply establishes your attitude of dwelling on things that you **will** do, rather than on things you plan to **try** with that built-in excuse in advance of possible failure.

3. Complete the following statements:

I enjoy _____

I am _____

I am learning _____

I like _____

I am an asset to _____

I will _____

I know I can _____

I am confident _____

4. Focus your attention and energy on the achievement of the objectives you are involved with right now, your *current dominant thoughts.*

   ❖ Forget about the consequences of failure.

   ❖ Remember you usually get what you think of most.

5. Listed below are things people say they want. Check the ones you would like to achieve. Then add others you've identified specifically for you. Disregard any fear of failure. Dream. *What do you really want?*

   become more self-confident _____

   feel comfortable in a crowd _____

   get involved in the environment _____

   have more energy _____

   manage time better _____

   eat more nutritious foods _____

   develop better listening skills _____

   earn more money _____

be appreciated at work　　　　———————————————

have people like and respect me　———————————————

lose weight　　　　　　　　———————————————

quit smoking　　　　　　　———————————————

develop financial security　　———————————————

relax at will　　　　　　　———————————————

develop my career　　　　　———————————————

develop better listening　　　———————————————

be more enthusiastic　　　　———————————————

overcome worry　　　　　　———————————————

get a job　　　　　　　　———————————————

succeed in school　　　　　———————————————

Others:　　　　　　　　　———————————————

　　　　　　　　　　　　　———————————————

　　　　　　　　　　　　　———————————————

6. Make a list of five of your most important current wants or desires. Beside each want or desire write your motive and the benefit there is to you when you achieve this want or desire. Look at this list before you go to bed each night and upon awakening each morning.

Want or Desire	Motive	Benefit
———————	———————	———————
———————	———————	———————
———————	———————	———————
———————	———————	———————

Positive Self-Motivation Action Reminders

Seek out and talk to a person who is currently doing what you want to do – someone who is doing this well

Find an expert

Get the facts

Learn everything you can about winners in your field

Take a course

Get personal lessons

Generate excitement by mentally seeing yourself enjoying the rewards of success

Guidelines for Positive Self-Talk

	Ineffective	Effective
Use personal pronouns Words such as "I", "my", "mine", and "me" will personalize your self-talk and help you internalize it.	People are fun to be around. Time is money.	I enjoy being around people. I am well-organized and
Keep your positve self-talk in the present tense. Referring to the past or future dilutes the impact of your self-talk.	Someday I'll be successful. I'm better disciplined than I used to be.	I am successful. I am well-disciplined.
Direct your positive self-talk toward what you desire, not away from what you don't want. You want to focus your current dominant thought on your desires, not your dislikes.	I can quit smoking. I won't worry anymore.	I am vice president, fully capable of fulfilling my responsibilities.
Keep your positive self-talk noncompetitive. Don't compare yourself with others.	I am in control of my habits. I am a confident, optimistic person who looks forward to each day	I will become vice president before he or she does.

POSITIVE SELF-AWARENESS

*A greater poverty than
that caused by money
is the poverty of unawareness*

Winners open their minds
to new opinions,
ideas, things, concepts,
and activities

AIMS

- ❖ To examine and understand *Positive Self-Awareness* through the exploration of environmental, physical, and mental situations

- ❖ To evaluate the ways you are able to adapt to environmental, physical, and mental situations

- ❖ To compile a list of positive occurrences in and around your life and to develop plans and actions for self-development

- ❖ To integrate *Positive Self-Awareness* into your personal and professional goals

VOCABULARY

Positive Self-Awareness	*Fight or Flight*
Environmental Self-Awareness	*Distress*
Empathy	*Invisible Entrapment*
Adaptability	*Racehorses*
Physical Self-Awareness	*Turtles*
Stress	*Mental Self-Awareness*

One of the most important Winner's elements for success is **Positive Self-Awareness**. Self-Awareness is the ability to step back from the canvas of life and take a good look at yourself as you relate to your environmental, physical, and mental world. Self-Awareness is the ability to accept yourself as a unique, imperfect, changing, and growing individual and to recognize your own vast potential as well as your limitations.

Positive Self-Awareness is self-honesty. Winners are honest not just with other people's money or confidences, but they are honest with themselves. Winners are honest about their potential and the time and effort necessary for top achievement. Winners can look in the mirror and see what lies behind their own eyes. You are a Winner when what you think, how you feel, and what you do are consistent. Winners are more sensitive than others around them. They don't need drugs or external stimulants to make life exciting. They are turned on naturally.

Positive Self- Awareness

Winners display a positive **Environmental Self-Awareness**. They are well aware of how little they really know about anything in their world and that what they do know is shaded by their own heredity and environment. Losers are unaware or unwilling to accept what is happening in their environments, unaware of the needs of others, and unaware of their own personal involvement with life.

Winners are eager to learn, especially about their own potential contribution to the quality of life. They are keenly aware of the abundance available to them. Losers become hardened, cold, and closed to new ideas and new opportunities. This hardness can range from intellectual cynicism, to indifference and apathy, to prejudice and aloofness, to vulgarity and rudeness. Losers are narrow-minded human beings. Winners are open. They see the many alternatives in every situation. They look at the relative rather than the absolute facts.

Are you open minded? Do you look at life through your parents' eyes? Are your prejudices inherited, or are they your own? Positive Environmental Self-Awareness is realizing that each human being on earth is a person with equal rights to fulfill his or her own potential in life. Positive Environmental Self-Awareness is realizing that skin

Environ- mental Awareness

color, birthplace, religious beliefs, sex, financial status, and intelligence are not measures of worth or worthiness. Positive Environmental Self-Awareness is accepting the fact that every human being is a distinctly unique individual. No two people are alike, not even identical twins.

Empathy

We speak at different frequencies and think at different frequencies. How many times have you heard people say, *"We're not on the same wavelength?"* We, in the human race, have been trying to get on the same wavelength for many centuries. No wonder there is so much discord in family, social, and international life. Everyone hears a different drummer, sees through a different lens, perceives through a different filter, and decides as a result of a different computer program in his or her own brain. **Empathy** is the understanding, awareness, and sensitivity of the feelings, thoughts, and experiences of another in a vicarious way.

❖ *Empathy is "feeling with" someone else.*

❖ *Empathy is watching the marathon runners at the 20-mile mark and having your own legs ache.*

❖ *Empathy is crawling into another person's being and looking at yourself through his or her eyes.*

Empathy may often have to be learned, as the following story illustrates: A woman took her five-year-old son shopping during the Christmas season. She knew he would enjoy all the decorations, window dressings, carol music, toys, and Santa Claus. Soon after they arrived, however, the boy began to cry softly and cling to his mother's coat. "Good grief, what are you fussing about?" she scolded. "Santa doesn't visit crybabies!"

She knelt down in the aisle beside him to tie his shoe, and as she knelt, she happened to look up. For the first time, she viewed her world through the eyes of a five-year-old! No stately Christmas trees, carefully strung garlands, or gaily decorated table displays – just a maze of aisles too high to see over, crowded with shoppers' legs and feet. From this view, things didn't seem like fun, just terribly confusing. She took her child right home and vowed never to impose her version of fun on him again. She was able to see through her five-year-old's eyes – she was able to empathize with him. The same goes for empathy with teenagers, young adults, foreigners, and others whose "view" you have not seen.

Give yourself the following Empathy Check-Up.

- ❖ *How would I like to have a partner like me if I were my spouse?*

- ❖ *How would I like to have a parent like me if I were my child?*

- ❖ *How would I like to have a student like me if I were the teacher?*

- ❖ *How would I like to have a manager like me if I were my employee?*

- ❖ *How does the world appear through the eyes of a child?*

- ❖ *How would it feel to be an immigrant newly arrived in America?*

Does it exasperate you to discover that there are so many weird people around compared to you? Did it ever occur to you that you may seem really weird to others, too? What is weird for certain? What is certain is that we need to understand what being human is, and that is a changing, growing, imperfect, but amazing living creation. Winners have that marvelous ability to understand their own relationship to their environments and to the many people and events that interact in everyday life.

Adaptability is the answer. By remaining open and flexible to the actions of others through our own empathy and self-awareness, we will not allow others to ruin our days with their bad days or to rain on our parades.

When we understand that there is tremendous abundance in the environment which we may have been viewing with a negative eye, we are ready to move inward to our own internal lifestyle. Our next step is to develop an attitude toward our **Physical Self-Awareness**.

Physical Awareness

Positive Physical Self-Awareness means we need to understand that our bodies are machines whose performance is largely dependent upon good health. We must treat our bodies as our one and only transportation vehicle for life with the high-test fuel of good nutrition, activity and health care. If we are fat and sluggish or gaunt and nervous because we smoke, drink excessively, lack exercise and/or eat poorly, we cannot trade in our bodies for a new model. If we abuse them, we won't be able to use them as long or as well. You can only do good if you feel good.

Stress

Stress is defined as a physical, chemical, or emotional effect that causes bodily or mental tension and may be a factor in causing disease. One of the best ways to develop adaptability to the stresses of life is to view them as normal. Earl Nightingale, a well-known motivationalist, tells of his visit with his son to the Great Barrier Reef which stretches nearly 1,800 miles from New Guinea to Australia. He noticed that the coral polyps on the inside of the reef, where the sea was tranquil and quiet in the lagoon, appeared pale and lifeless, while the coral on the outside of the reef, subject to the surge of the tide and power of the waves, were bright and vibrant with splendid colors and flowing growth. Earl asked his guide why this was so. *"It's very simple,"* came the reply. *"The coral on the lagoon side dies rapidly with no challenge for growth and survival, while the coral facing the open sea thrives and multiplies because it is challenged and tested every day."* And so it is with every living organism on earth. The adversity and failures in our lives, if adapted and viewed as normal corrective feedback, serve to develop in us an immunity against anxiety, depression, and the adverse response to stress.

Little has changed since the days of our early ancestors when – at the first hint of a dangerous or threatening confrontation – the body automatically mustered its defenses in preparation for **Fight or Flight**. Man would either defend him/herself or flee. Instead of a sabre-tooth-tiger-a-week or a dinosaur-a-month, today it is at least one or two unwelcome or unpleasant interpersonal surprises almost every day.

How many complete strangers got you upset and ready to risk your life on the road today? Losers in life overreact to what is happening, like cave dwellers. They flare to anger quickly and get defensive easily. Their blood pressure jumps, their heart rate quickens, their arteries constrict, and the adrenalin pumps. They rush headlong into an imaginary struggle for survival as if they are running and hiding from imaginary predators and volcanic eruptions. The effects of this type of daily **distress** or negative stress are devastating to the mental and physical health of the individual. As a result, the Loser drinks more, smokes mores, frets more, and pops more pills to cope or escape.

Anti-anxiety drugs serve to reduce emotional reactions to the threat of pain or failure; that is why they are taken. But unfortunately, they also interfere with the ability to learn to tolerate these stresses. Dr. Robert Eliot, member of the Board of Governors of the American College of Cardiology and President of the International Stress Foundation, has studied the relationship between stress and heart attacks, strokes, and other diseases of today. Dr. Eliot refers to the syndrome of **"invisible entrapment,"** or deep-seated worries, frustrations, and anxieties of people unable to cope effectively with their changing status in a changing world, as major factors in the increasing incidence of sudden death from heart attacks and other mental and physical illnesses. While we are in the process of winning the battle against infectious diseases attacking us from outside ourselves, we seem to be losing ground to those that result from our own inner conflicts.

Positive Self-Awareness is one important part of the ultimate victory over stress. It is far better to develop behavioral methods of coping with one's problems than to dissolve them with a pill. This is an important element of *Positive Self-Awareness*: Winners learn how to relax and cope with the trials and tribulations of everyday life, without amphetamines when they are depressed, or tranquilizers when they are anxious. Dr. Hans Selye in Montreal, acknowledged world pioneer of early stress research, has suggested in his books and interviews that each individual should try to find his or her own healthy stress level in life and operate within that level. He generally categorizes us as **"racehorses"** or **"turtles"** by nature. A racehorse loves to run and will die from exhaustion if it is corralled and confined, while a turtle will die from exhaustion if forced to run on a treadmill, moving too fast for its own unique step-by-step nature.

While expressing emotions such as love, joy, compassion, and exhilaration is healthy and desirable, it may be beneficial to us if we can minimize the overt expression of hostility, anger, depression, loneliness, and anxiety. The only healthy expression of the Fight or Flight emotion is in the face of a life or death situation. In most of our daily confrontations, hostility and anger can be dealt with by deep breathing, relaxation, and an exercise program involving activities such as running, aerobics, or tennis. If we want to conquer undesirable emotional tendencies in ourselves, we must learn to go through the outward movements of the desirable, positive dispositions that we prefer to cultivate.

Mental Awareness

An important element of *Positive Self-Awareness* is **Mental Self-Awareness**, that knowledge of the potential and abundance within our own minds which waits to be challenged. Dr. William James, a recognized leader in early psychology, said that even the most effective humans utilize less than ten percent of their mental potential. We should ask: *"What is my mental outlook toward myself in life? Have I been selling myself short, or have I been overconfident in my abilities?"*

The pursuit of mind-expanding techniques toward a heightened state of awareness has been a mysterious journey beginning, perhaps, in the high mountains of Tibet. Today, the quest for Mental Self-Awareness ranges from the ridiculous to the sublime, from alpha brain wave simulators, to biorhythms, to horoscopes, to quiet meditation. The interesting point about all these mind-expanding experiences is that the effects of these may soon wear off and we'll go back to our original selves. About the only thing we've usually gained is a little more disillusionment and a little more confusion about the real answers to life.

Attitude is the *key* to *Positive Self-Awareness.* In order to feel well mentally and to do good in the world, you need to get your head together through constructive thinking, not through lip service, nor through one self-awareness cult after another, but by dedicated learning of new, healthy responses to the stimuli of life.

We must seek and walk with truth every day of our lives and always be open to different alternatives and better ways to win. The foundation upon which every fulfilled life has been built includes the three cornerstones of truth, integrity, and honesty. They must be present for any real and lasting success of any kind. To be a healthy human being, with *Positive Self-Awareness* under every circumstance, is to ask ourselves, *"Is this true?" "Is this honest?"* If we can answer *"Yes,"* or if we can seek the truth from someone who has experienced it, we can move ahead to action. Winners with this awareness are sensitive to the needs and differences of others, aware that the clock is always running, knowing that *there is still time to Win.*

REVIEW

Read this Positive Self-Awareness Review several times over the period of one month to etch it in your memory.

Winners know who they are, what they believe, the role in life they are now filling, their great personal potential – and the future roles and goals which will mark fulfillment of that potential. They have learned these things, and are constantly adding to their knowledge through experience, insight, feedback, and judgment. As a result they can continuously not only "play for strength" in the game of life, but also avoid errors and correct weaknesses. Their judgments are characterized by extreme honesty. They don't kid others and they don't kid themselves. *Losers* say, "Who knows what I could do if someone gave me a chance." *Winners* say, "I know who I am, where I'm coming from, and where I'm going."

Make this moment the moment of truth about yourself. You have the opportunity to experience more environmental, physical, and mental abundance than you could use in several lifetimes. Open up your eyes to the possibilities and alternatives available in your life. Change your attitude and your lifestyle and your many environments will change automatically. Understand your own uniqueness. Appreciate the differences in others. Relax and learn to respond positively to stress. Change for the better that which can be changed. Remove from your life or adapt to those negative influences that cannot be changed.

Thought-Provoking Questions

1. What is the key to *Positive Self-Awareness*? Explain how it affects your self-development.

2. How many complete strangers got you upset and/or ready to risk your life on the road today? Why do we let this happen? Why do others aggravate us? How can we prevent this?

3. What is the first step in self-development?

4. Why is the person who does not read no better than the person who cannot read, or the person who does not continue to learn, adapt, and grow no better than the one who cannot?

5. Recall a situation involving empathy with another person. How do you know you empathized with that person? What were your emotions? How did you feel?

6. How can you develop yourself through *Positive Environmental Self-Awareness*? *Positive Physical Self-Awareness*? *Positive Mental Self-Awareness*?

7. Recall the characterization of a "racehorse" and a "turtle." Which one are you? Why? Give an example of a situation.

Strategies for Achieving Self-Awareness

1. Be more curious about everything in your world.

    ❖ *Read the newspaper*

    ❖ *Read best-sellers*

    ❖ *Watch informational TV*

    ❖ *Attend seminars and lectures*

    ❖ *Seek out and gain counsel from the most successful people you know*

2. Be empathetic; learn how others feel and consider where they are coming from before criticizing or passing judgment.

3. Seek out and listen to the opinions and reactions of everyone around you, including children and the elderly. Their perspectives can be enlightening.

4. Schedule an annual medical and dental examination.

5. Break the daily and weekly routine you have set for yourself.

    ❖ *Get out of that comfortable rut*

    ❖ *Unplug the television for a week*

    ❖ *Go to classes or work using a different route or by another mode of transportation*

    ❖ *Instead of reaching for a beer, take a walk*

6. Use the following chart to list your best traits and then the traits that need improvement. In the last column, list an improvement activity.

Best Traits	Traits to Improve	Activity to Improve
_____	_____	_____
_____	_____	_____
_____	_____	_____
_____	_____	_____

6

POSITIVE SELF-ESTEEM

If you love yourself,
then you can give love
How can you give what you
don't have?

The success of others
has nothing to do with
your success,
nor is your success
measured by what others
say or what
others accomplish

AIMS

❖ To define *Positive Self-Esteem* as it relates to *Winners* and *Losers*

❖ To create and employ strategies for developing *Positive Self-Esteem*

❖ To practice *Positive Self-Talk* as it relates to *Positive Self-Esteem*

❖ To recall and relate past successes to develop *Positive Self-Esteem*

❖ To identify past defeats and incorporate them in the development of *Positive Self-Esteem*

VOCABULARY

Positive Self-Esteem   *Permanent Potential*

Self-Esteem   *Emotions*

Social Slights   *Self-Acceptance*

Esteem

Positive Self-Esteem means accepting yourself the way you are at this moment and basing your actions and decisions on rational thinking rather than emotion. *Positive Self-Esteem* is one of the most important and basic qualities of a winning human being. It is that deep-down, inside-the-skin feeling of your own worth that leads to achievement and happiness. *"You know, I like myself. I really do like myself. I'm glad I'm me. I'd rather be me than anyone else living or at any other time in history."* This is the self-talk of a Winner, and Positive Self-Talk is important to developing **self-esteem**, the confidence and satisfaction in one's self so important to all of us. Winners develop strong beliefs of self-worth and self-confidence. They weren't necessarily born with these good feelings, but as with every other habit, they have learned to like themselves through practice.

Some individuals are born with much more going for them at the start. Many children, in their early years, have been encouraged and nurtured by winning parents, outstanding teachers, coaches, and friends who gave them early feelings of self-esteem. This is perhaps the most important quality of a good parent or a good business leader – positive encouragement toward the development of self-worth.

Unfortunately, some of the offspring of the richest, most beautiful, most prominent and talented people have become Losers, unable to live up to their heritage and unable to accept themselves or perform effectively in society. This may be because they had so much going for them at the start that they developed no inner drive to take them forward. Yet, some children from the most backward, discouraging beginnings have grown into outstanding Winners and top achievers in every walk of life. Out of adversity can come greatness.

As we were growing up, many of us played an inferior role to the adults in our lives. We were told what to do and what not to do. We were constantly reminded of our shortcomings in phrases such as, *"Don't interrupt, children should be seen and not heard!" "You're not old enough to do that!" "You should know that by now."* This bombardment can take its toll, and if practiced continually can create troubled teens and divide children from parents or students from teachers.

As we grow to adulthood, this role causes us to walk a tightrope between humility, which is a good trait, and humiliation, which is not good. Losers allow humiliation to become a driving force in their lives. Winners develop humility, accepting correction graciously, learning from errors, and maintaining perspective. To develop an even higher degree of *Positive Self-Esteem*, Winners learn to understand that self-development is a lifetime program.

Low achievers water and cultivate these early seeds of inferior feelings with their imaginations and develop a strong prickly weed of low self-esteem which sticks and irritates for years to come. Those who yell the loudest are really calling for help because of low self-esteem. What they are really shouting is: *"Help, look at me, please!"*

When we examine Losers and low-achievers, an attitude of low self-esteem seems to be at the root of their problems. Studies of aircraft skyjackers and assassins have shown that these aggressors are very likely to be loners with extremely low self-esteem. The same is true with most criminals.

Psychiatrist Bernard Holland has pointed out that although juvenile delinquents appear to be very independent and have a reputation of being braggarts, particularly about how they hate everyone in authority, they protest too much. Underneath this hard exterior shell, says Dr. Holland, *"is a soft vulnerable inner person who wants to be dependent upon others."* However, they cannot get close to anyone because they will not trust anyone. At some time in the past they were hurt by a person important to them, and they dare not leave themselves open to be hurt again. They must always have their defenses up. To prevent further rejection and pain, they attack first. Thus, they drive away the very people who would love them, if given half a chance, and could help them. This description also applies to many people with whom we associate who are not juvenile delinquents. They may be peers or even loved ones.

Many people we know are hurt terribly by **social slights**, those offending remarks or actions, intentional or not, that occur publicly. Often, the people who become offended the easiest have the lowest self-esteem. The people who feel undeserving, doubt their own capabilities, and have a poor opinion of themselves become jealous very easily. Jealousy, which is the scourge of many relationships, is nearly always caused by self-doubt. The person with adequate self-esteem doesn't feel hostile toward others, isn't out to prove anything, can see the facts more clearly, and isn't demanding in his or her claims on other people.

Bernard Baruch, a famous American businessman and statesman, was once asked how he went about arranging the seating of guests for his dinner parties without offending anybody. He replied that he solved the problem by simply allowing his guests to seat themselves, choosing where they wished to sit. As he put it, *"The people who matter don't mind, and the people who mind . . . don't matter."* The principle that Baruch uncovered is true in all walks of life. Those who know who they are need not be defensive – nor do they have to go out of their way to prove anything. Their solid self-esteem is quite enough to get them anywhere they want to go.

The word **esteem** literally means "to appreciate value or worth." Why do we stand in awe of the power and immensity of the sea, the uniqueness of a solar eclipse, the beauty of a flower, a giant redwood, or a sunset, and at the same time, downgrade ourselves? Don't downgrade the product just because you haven't used it properly and effectively. We are all able to think, experience, and love. It would be impossible to love another person without first feeling love for yourself, because how could you give away something that you don't have? It is important to develop the deep-down, inside-the-skin feeling of deserving the abundance. Self-esteem is felt even though you may not have done anything yet, but just feel the capability for it.

Many people have a negative attitude about personal development. On the one hand, they know that learning brings about change, but on the other hand, they resist change. They know that many people have overcome enormous obstacles to become great, but they can't imagine it happening to them. And so they resign themselves to be the "also-rans" in life, wishing and envying away their lives. These lowachievers learn the habit of concentrating on their failures and the negative events in their lives with self-talk that reinforces the losing cycle.

Permanent Potential

Because they are controlled by external standards set by others, they often set their sights too high and are unrealistic. As they fail to reach their goals again and again, these failures become set in their subconscious self-images as targets and goals of their own. This explains why so many people have **permanent potential**, that untapped ability for sustained success. In other words, why they *almost* succeed over and over, having temporary, fleeting successes, which fail to materialize into a solid lifestyle.

Winners Reinforce Past Successes

Confidence is built upon the experience of success. When we begin anything new we usually have little confidence because we have not learned from experience that we can succeed. This is as true with learning to ride a bicycle as it is with leading people. It is true that success breeds success. Winners focus on past successes and forget past failures. They use errors and mistakes as a vehicle for learning – then they dismiss them from their minds.

Yet, what do many of us do? We destroy our self-confidence by remembering past failures and forgetting all about our past successes. We not only remember failures, we etch them in our minds with emotion. We condemn ourselves. Winners know that it doesn't matter how many times they have failed in the past. It's their successes which should be remembered, reinforced, and dwelt upon.

To establish true self-esteem, we must concentrate on our successes and look at the failures and negatives in our lives only as corrective feedback to get us on target again. The child's view must be recognized as serving a purpose in early years, but we must drop it aside as we mature. Instead of comparing ourselves to others, we should view ourselves in terms of our own abilities, interests, and goals. We can begin by making a conscious effort to upgrade our lifestyle and personal habits.

Positive Self-Esteem is then developed by basing more of our actions and decisions on rational thinking rather than on emotions. **Emotions** are automatic, subconscious reactions. To respond to the daily experiences and challenges of life by reacting emotionally is to nullify the wisdom and power of the rational mind. Winners are able to enjoy their emotions – like children probing the depths of love, excitement, joy, and compassion; but they make the decisions that shape their lives through logic and common sense. Relationships today would be much stronger if they were entered into intelligently, as well as emotionally.

To develop and maintain our self-esteem we need to find pleasure and pride in where we are rather than looking for greener pastures elsewhere. This is the philosophy of mining your "Acres of Diamonds"* right now, right where you are – making changes in your internal reactions rather than searching for external stimulation in a new environment.

Although we are always seeking improvement, the Winner with *Positive Self-Esteem* can accept himself or herself just as he or she is at this moment. Since the perfect human has not been discovered, we all need to live with our hang-ups and idiosyncracies until they can be ironed out. One of the most important aspects of self-esteem that accounts for successful, dynamic living is that of **self-acceptance** – the willingness to be oneself and live one's life as it is unfolding, accepting all responsibility for the ultimate outcome. Shakespeare explained it when, in *Hamlet*, he had Polonius say:

> *And this above all, to thine own self be true – and it must follow as the night the day – thou can'st not then be false, to any man.*

Remember, the most important key to the permanent enhancement of self-esteem is the practice of Positive Self-Talk. Every waking moment we must feed our subconscious positive thoughts about ourselves and our performances so relentlessly and vividly that our self-images are in time modified to conform to the new, higher standards.

Research on the effect of words and images on the functions of the body offers amazing evidence of the power that words, spoken at random, can have on body functions monitored on biofeedback

Positive Self-Talk Is the Key

*"Acres of Diamonds" is the title of a lecture given hundreds of times by Russell Herman Conwell (1843 - 1925), the founder and first president of Temple University. The essence of his lecture was that opportunity lies at our own doorstep.

equipment. Since thoughts can raise and lower body temperature, secrete hormones, relax muscles and nerve endings, dilate and constrict arteries, and raise and lower pulse rate, it is obvious that we need to control the language we use on ourselves. That's why Winners rarely "put themselves down" in actions or in words. Losers fall into the trap of saying: *"I can't," "I wish," "Yeah, but,"* and *"I should have."* Winners use constructive feedback and self-talk every day: *"I can," "I look forward," "Next time, I'll get it right,"* and *"I'm feeling better."*

One good indicator of an individual's opinion of himself or herself is the way he or she can accept a compliment. It is incredible how lowachievers belittle and demean themselves when others try to pay them value:

"Your oral report was really good."
"Yeah, but Jim's was better."
"I'd like to congratulate you on a job well done."
"Oh, it was nothing . . . I was just lucky, I guess."
"Wow, that was a great shot you made!"
"Yeah, I had my eyes closed."
"That's a good looking suit."
"This old thing? I've had it forever."

The Loser's robot self-image is always listening and accepts these negative statements as fact. On the other hand, Winners in life accept compliments by simply saying *"thank you"* because *Positive Self-Esteem* is the quality of accepting value that is paid to you by others.

In studies of Winners who have pulled themselves up and who remain at the top in life, a high self-esteem seems to be the common denominator. Almost without exception, the real Winners, whether we speak of sports, business, or any other activity in life, have accepted their own uniqueness, feel comfortable with their image, and are willing to have others know and accept them just as they are. It is an interesting fact that such people naturally attract friends and supporters. They seldom have to stand alone.

Winners know that contrary to popular belief this feeling of self-acceptance and deserving is not necessarily a legacy from wise and loving parents. History is full of saints who rose from the gutters.

Recognizing their own uniqueness, they develop and maintain their own high standards. Winners are aware of their potential. They like who they are. Since they have a deep feeling of their own worth, they are eager to love others as they do themselves. *Positive Self-Esteem –* one of the most important qualities of a Winner. *Talk yourself up!*

REVIEW

Read this Positive Self-Esteem Review several times over the period of one month to etch it in your memory.

Winners have a deep-down feeling of their own worth. They know that, contrary to popular belief, this feeling of self-acceptance and deserving is not necessarily a legacy from wise and loving parents – history is full of saints who rose from the gutters. *Winners* are not outer-directed. Recognizing their uniqueness, they develop and maintain their own high standards. Though they recognize the universality of fear and anxiety, *Winners* don't give in to these emotions. Losing self-talk: *"I'd rather be somebody else."* Winning self-talk: *"I do things well because I'm that kind of person."*

Accept yourself as you are right now – an imperfect, changing, growing, and worthwhile person. Realize that liking yourself and feeling that you're a super individual in your own special way is not necessarily egotistical. In addition to taking pride in what you are accomplishing, enjoy the unique person that you are just being alive right now. Understand that although we as individuals are not all born with equal attributes, we are born with equal rights to feel the excitement and joy in believing that we deserve the very best in life. Most successful people believe in their own worth, even when they have nothing to hold on to but a dream. Perhaps more than any other quality, *healthy self-esteem is the door to high achievement and happiness.*

Thought-Provoking Questions

1. Some people feel good about themselves. They seem to project an attitude of self-confidence and belief in themselves. They are comfortable with who they are. Others lack self-esteem. They are uncomfortable with themselves because they feel unworthy or inadequate. Discuss how self-esteem, or lack of it, can affect one's life.

    ❖ Studies of skyjackers, assassins, and other criminals have shown that these people have little self-esteem. What does this tell you about the importance of self-esteem?

    ❖ The feelings we have about ourselves are often developed at an extremely early age. One research project revealed that, between the ages of one and fifteen, children normally hear between 15,000 and 25,000 times: *"no," "don't," "you can't," "better not,"* and *"shouldn't."* What do you feel we can do to overcome this negative input and increase our own and other's self-esteem?

    ❖ One way to establish true self-esteem is to focus your attention on your success and positive experience. Practice *"focusing on the positives"* by sharing a success you've had. Take turns telling the others something you've accomplished about which you feel especially good.

    ❖ Another way to establish true self-esteem is to look at your failures and negative experiences in a constructive way, as corrective feedback that will get you on target again. Has anyone in your group been able to turn a failure experience into a positive learning experience? Please share this experience with your group members.

2. People resist change even when they know it is for their benefit. What specifically do they do to concentrate on their failures, on what has happened in the past? How can this phenomenon be turned around to our benefit?

3. Juvenile delinquents appear to be very independent but are in actuality lacking trust. At what point does this occur? Why do our thresholds differ? Can we be proactive in this process?

4. Relationships today would be much stronger if they were entered into intelligently, as well as emotionally. What do we look for in relationships? Do emotions overrule?

Strategies for Achieving Positive Self-Esteem

1. Keep a self-development plan at all times. Commit it to paper:

   ❖ *Knowledge you will require*
   ❖ *Behavior you will require*
   ❖ *Changes in your life that will result*

2. Take stock today of your good reasons for self-esteem. Write down your "**BAG**": Blessings Accomplishments Goals

   Blessings: *You are thankful to whom and for what?*

   Accomplishments: *What have you done about which you are proud?*

   Goals: *What are your dreams and ambitions?*

Positive Self-Esteem
Daily Affirmations

I see the abundance and wonder all around me.

I am a worthy human being, enjoying a deep down feeling of value and self-worth.

I am in control of my life. I react to all problems and situations with calm assurance.

I am a motivated individual, fully capable of reaching my goals.

I expect the very best.

I know who I am, what I stand for, and what I believe.

7

POSITIVE SELF-PROJECTION

*How you walk, talk,
listen, and look
is You*

*The only limits to
your accomplishments in
life are self-imposed*

AIMS

- ❖ To evaluate your projection to others

- ❖ To develop and practice good listening skills

- ❖ To identify and interpret nonverbal communication signals

- ❖ To employ the KISS formula

- ❖ To produce a plan of *Positive Self-Projection* and set that plan into action

VOCABULARY

Positive Self-Projection   *KISS Formula*

Encode   *Active Listening*

Sender   *Nonverbal Communication*

Receiver

Communication

Winners in life are walking examples of **Positive Self-Projection**, they have an aura of success and confidence. While the qualities of *Positive Self-Projection* – strong communication skills and good appearance are, in part, the natural result of *Positive Self-Esteem*, Winners know that nothing just happens, and work to *make* things happen. They are aware of all aspects of self-projection and use this knowledge to develop their image in all personal encounters.

Winners know that everyone projects and receives through a different communication system. Often the receiver of a message will need to **encode** the information: that is, he or she will convert the message to that which is understandable.

People, whether they know it or not, telegraph their intentions and feelings. They become **senders**. Whatever goes on inside shows outside. **Receivers** absorb most of these nonverbal communications below the conscious level of thinking. Our subconscious, robot-like minds will encode these messages based on past experience.

Winners in business or personal relationships take full responsibility for success in the communication process. In other words, Winners never meet you half-way or go fifty-fifty. As talkers, Winners take full responsibility for being certain that you understand what they are saying. By giving examples, by asking you for feedback, by putting what they said in different words, they make it easy for you to gain the true intent of their communications.

Winners use the **KISS Formula**. *KISS* in communications means "*Keep It Straightforward and Simple.*" Winners know that everyone interprets what he or she hears and sees differently. Winners project in clear, concise, simple language and use words and examples that don't evoke a double meaning or hidden agenda.

Winners learn the art of projecting themselves through **active listening**. Once they introduce themselves they become listeners. They know that listeners learn a great deal while talkers learn nothing. Again, they *take responsibility* for hearing what you mean. Winners ask questions, they draw the other person out, they ask for examples, they ask others to put it in other words, and they feed back what others have just said for clarity and understanding. Winners know that giving value to others is the greatest communication skill of all.

When Winners face a prospect, an adversary, a potential friend, or when they pick up a telephone, their attitude is service-oriented, not self-oriented. Their concern is for the other person, not themselves. When we have someone else's interest at heart, not just our own, the other person can sense it. That person may not be able to put into words why he or she feels that way, but only that the feeling exists. On the other hand, people get an uneasy feeling when they talk with a person who has only his or her own interests in mind and not theirs.

Nonverbal Communication

Think back to the people who have had the most influence on you. You'll likely find that they were people who really cared about you – your parents, a fine teacher, a business associate, a good friend – someone who was interested in you. The only people you will influence to any great degree will be the people you care about. When you are with people you care about, their interest, not yours, will be uppermost in your mind. Our success in getting along with others and communicating effectively with them depends upon this same principle. It depends solely upon our ability to help other people solve their problems. This is *Positive Self-Projection.* Winners say, *"I'll make you glad you talked to me."* And you'll know you're a true Winner in the game of life when you hear this statement often from those you meet: *"I like me best when I'm with you."*

There's an excellent reason why we all get these feelings about people. It's known as **nonverbal communication**: the body language, facial expressions, and gestures that often signal our thoughts and feelings more clearly than our actual words. In his book, *Nonverbal Communications*, Dr. Jurgen Ruesch, Professor of Psychiatry at the University of California, says that we communicate by means of some seven hundred thousand nonverbal signals. It's easy to understand why nonverbal communication has more effect than most of us realize.

Winners listen to the total person. They observe body language, realizing that folded or crossed arms sometimes mean a defensive or introverted listener. They understand that hands on the hips or active gesturing may mean an aggressive attitude. Winners watch the eyes which can look down or away in self-consciousness or guilt or which can flare in surprise or anger. Winners listen to the extra-verbal messages: tone of voice; nervous laughter; rehearsed, unemotional monotone, or rapid, excited chatter.

Winners in life project constructive, supportive ideas. Winners are neither cynical nor critical. Winners accept another viewpoint as being valid even if it is completely opposed to their own beliefs. A Winner says, *"I appreciate and understand your position. However, I would like to tell you why my position may be different from your own."*

When Will Rogers, the cowboy philosopher of the 1920s, said, *"I never met a man I didn't like,"* he didn't mean he approved of all the traits and characteristics of every person he met. What he did find was something he could admire in everyone. We get back from people what we give them. If we want to be loved, we must first be lovable.

You can always spot a Winner when he or she first enters a room. Winners project an aura; they have an unmistakable presence, a charisma which is disarming, radiating, and magnetic. They project that warm glow that comes from the inside. What they project naturally is their Positive Self-Esteem.

You never have a second chance to make a first impression. Winners have learned through experience that people project and respond to a gut-level feeling, which is nearly instantaneous. They are aware that first impressions are powerful and lasting, and they know the elements necessary to evoke a positive first impression.

Four minutes is all it takes to project a positive or negative first impression. Many careers, top jobs, sales deals, and other important transactions are decided very early in the interview or negotiations based on "gut feelings" and self-projection. How you project yourself when meeting someone for the first time is very important and involves direct eye contact, a smile, handshake, and good listening skills.

The Critical First Impression

Project Self-Worth

Most importantly, self-esteem is transmitted with a smile, which is the universal language that opens doors, melts defenses, and saves a thousand words. A smile is the light in your window that tells others there is a caring, sharing person inside.

Positive Self-Projection is the way in which we introduce ourselves to others. Winners, in a first encounter, whether in person or by telephone, usually lead by giving their own name first. As simple as it may seem, by stating our own name up front in a positive, affirmative manner, we are projecting self-worth and giving others immediate reason to accept us as someone to remember.

Winners get in touch by extending their hand first, knowing that it is the time-proven way of giving value to others. In ancient times, the handshake was a double-hand clasp, a way of showing that a weapon was not being concealed. Anyone who would not shake hands willingly was regarded with suspicion. Along with the warm handshake, Winners use direct eye contact to project interest in communication.

We need to respect the fact that we usually project on the outside how we really feel about ourselves on the inside. For example, when we aren't feeling well physically, we don't look well on the surface level. And, correspondingly, when we don't feel good about ourselves, emotionally or mentally, we don't seem to make a very good impression with our looks, personal grooming, and clothing habits.

A study performed by Harvard University pointed out that people who feel unattractive, as judged by themselves and their peers, tend to suffer from feelings of loneliness, rejection, and isolation. Schoolchildren who look good, that is, those who are clean and neat, are actually treated better, not only by their classmates but by their teachers as well. Other studies have shown that some of the most beautiful people, physically, are less satisfied, less well-adjusted, and less happy in later life.

William Thourlby, author of *You Are What You Wear - the Key to Business Success,* says that when you step into a room, even though no one in that room knows you or has seen you before, they will make certain decisions about you based solely on your appearance. Some of the likely judgments may be your:

Economic Level
Educational Level
Trustworthiness
Social Position
Level of Sophistication
Success
Moral Character

What can we learn from these insights? First, while we have no choice over the genes we have inherited, it is to our advantage to take care of our health and appearance and to do what we can to enhance what we've got. Like it or not, we are often judged by our appearance, which leaves a lasting impression. Second, since we behave in accordance with the way we *think* we look rather than the way we *actually* look to others, those of us who can learn to be satisfied with ourselves are way ahead of the game as far as being real Winners in life.

"Status" Symbols

There is a growing tendency among many individuals to flaunt expensive possessions and outward trappings of affluence. This focus on status symbols may really indicate that the owner is lacking self-esteem and needs to demonstrate importance with "things." It may be true that only those with a strong sense of self-worth can afford to display a modest image to the community when, in fact, they have much wealth. In other words, Winners can project success without flaunting it. Winners may not always be able to afford to buy the most expensive things, but they always do the very best with what they can afford.

There is a real need for rational values when we consider the true meaning of *Positive Self-Projection*. Sometimes we seem to be taking a good thing, which is "doing the best with what we've got," and going overboard with excessive self-adoration and self-indulgence in an attempt to buy superficial happiness. We mistakenly think that the kind of house, car, clothing, and possessions we show off to the world tells others who we are.

In our world of easy credit – in what some have called the "plastic age" because of the flood of credit cards and the ease with which they can be obtained and used – almost anyone can arrange to show off a fancy car or boat in front of their home. Unfortunately, the tendency to show off many toys and trappings of affluence and material success is more likely to project to others that we are really lacking in self-esteem or self-worth.

There are some fundamental, consistent patterns that winning human beings follow. Winners make good use of their minds, skills, and talent, and these become apparent in their lives. They project self-respect and respect for others in communication, and *Positive Self-Esteem* in their manner and appearance. These patterns define that aura of success and confidence which is *Positive Self-Projection. Project yourself every day as a Winner.*

REVIEW

Read this Positive Self-Projection review several times over the period of one month to etch it in your memory.

Winners practice *Positive Self-Projection.* They project their best selves every day in the way they look, walk, talk, listen, and react. They specialize in truly effective communication, taking complete responsibility not only for sending information or telling, but also for receiving information or listening for the real meaning from every person they contact. *Winners* are aware that first impressions are powerful, and that interpersonal relationships can be won or lost in the first four minutes of conversation. *Winners* say "I'll make them glad they talked with me." To a *Winner* you'll say "I like me best when I'm with you."

Nothing marks a *Winner* so clearly as a relaxed smile and a volunteer of a name, while extending a hand to yours, looking directly in your eyes, and showing interest in you by asking questions about your life which are important to you. *Winners* know that giving value to others is the greatest communication skill of all. A *Winner's* self-talk: *"Tell me what you want, maybe we can work on it together."*

Thought-Provoking Questions

1. Explain why the game of poker is a time when a player with a great hand of cards needs to be a receiver of information and not a sender.

2. Quite often when we meet another person or encounter a new situation, there is a gut reaction that occurs that is nearly instantaneous and may influence the outcome. What external clues about that person affect our gut reaction?

3. Do you create a positive first impression? List the personal projection factors that make your first impression a good one.

4. Personal appearance does not only mean our grooming habits. There are other factors involved in projecting a total image. What are they and how does each affect a good appearance?

5. Do you feel attractive? Why or why not? Do some clothes make you feel more attractive than others? What can you do to rid yourself of those things that make you feel unattractive?

6. Do you stand taller and walk straighter when you have a suit on rather than jeans and a T-shirt? If your goal is to project a winning attitude on the outside as well as from within, what can you do about it?

7. Using negative self-esteem, discuss how interpersonal relationships can be lost during the first four minutes of conversation.

8. Using Positive Self-Esteem, discuss how professional relationships can be won during the first four minutes of conversation.

9. If *Winners* project success without flaunting it, what characteristics do they portray? Intangibles? Tangibles?

Strategies for Achieving Self-Projection

1. What do you need to do to project your best self at all times?

2. Is there any change of clothing or appearance which will benefit you and your career? If so, list these changes.

3. With whom do you need to communicate more often? Use the chart below to schedule this communication.

People	Times

4. List the ways to improve your methods of communicating (*looking people in the eye, clarity of speech, etc*).

_____

_____

_____

_____

5. I need to be a better listener to the following people:

_____   _____

_____   _____

_____   _____

6. Use the following chart to establish new relationships.

Contact	Objective	Call	Appointment
With whom do I want a relationship?	What am I asking, and what do I have to offer?	Date/Time Phone Number	When/Where/ With Whom

Self-Projection Action Reminders

Here are some action reminders to help develop Positive Self-Projection

1. Dress and look your best at all times. Personal grooming and appearance provide a clear sign of your self-esteem.

2. Volunteer your own name first in every telephone call and whenever you meet someone new. By giving value to your own name in communication, you are developing the habit of giving value to yourself as an individual.

3. Respond with a simple, courteous *"thank you"* when anyone pays you a compliment for any reason.

4. Sit up front when you attend class, meetings, lectures, and conferences. Your purpose for going is to listen, learn, and possibly exchange questions and answers with the instructor or speaker. Don't lose yourself in a crowd.

5. Walk and stand tall. People who walk erectly and briskly usually are confident about themselves and where they are going.

6. Set your own internal standards rather than comparing yourself to others. Keep upgrading your own standards in life: behavior, professional accomplishment, relationships, etc.

7. Use encouraging, affirmative language when you talk to yourself and to others about yourself. Focus on positive words. Everything you say about yourself is subconsciously being recorded by others and, more importantly, by your own self-image.

8. Smile! In every language, in every culture , it is the light in your window that tells people there's a caring, sharing individual inside. It's the universal code for "I'm O.K. – you're O.K."

8

POSITIVE SELF-CONTROL

Life is a do-it-yourself project

We become what we think
about most of the time

AIMS

❖ To develop the skill of *Postitive Self-Control* , which puts you in control of your career, environment, and life

❖ To state your responsibilities to yourself, others, and society

❖ To engage in an honest appraisal of your own self-control

❖ To exert control over at least one aspect of your life and make it happen

❖ To list cause and effect relationships and examine your *Postitive Self-Control*

VOCABULARY

Positive Self-Control   *Personal Responsibility*

Self-Molded   *Law of Cause and Effect*

The true meaning of self-control is often misunderstood. Many people interpret self-control as "getting a good grip on yourself" or remaining cool and passive under pressure. **Positive Self-Control** is synonymous with self-determination. Winners with *Positive Self-Control* take full responsibility for determining their actions in their own lives. They have the philosophy that life is a "do-it-yourself" program. Self-control implies freedom for individuals to choose among many alternatives and to shape their own destinies.

Some people believe that fate, luck, an astrological sign, or some other force not in their control has shaped the outcome of their lives. People who feel that life is mostly determined by circumstances, predestination, or being in the right place at the right time are more likely to give in to doubt and fear. Those who cannot make up their minds for fear of making the wrong choice, vacillating in indecision, simply do not achieve their goals – a requirement for success. Rather, they take their place among the rank and file of the also-rans, trudging along in bland mediocrity. People who are aware that they exert control over what happens to them in life are happier and are able to choose more appropriate responses to whatever occurs.

Winners Take Control

All individuals are what they are – and where they are – as a composite result of all their own doings. They have shaped their own destinies and are **self-molded**. Although our innate characteristics and environments are given to us initially, the decisions we make determine whether we win or lose our particular game of life. Voltaire, a French writer of the 1700s, likened life to a game of cards. Each player must accept the cards life deals. Once the cards are in hand, he or she alone must decide how to play them in order to win the game.

The writer, John Erskine, put it a little differently when he wrote: *"Though we sometimes speak of a primrose path, we all know that a bad life is just as difficult, just as full of work, obstacles, and hardships, as a good one. The only choice is the kind of life one would care to spend one's efforts on."* Whether you are a bum on skid row or a happy individual – you can pat yourself on the back, taking the credit or the blame for your place in life. You took over control from your parents when you were very young and have been in the driver's seat ever since. Many children

Who Are We?

learn how to control their parents' lives, long before they know how to talk in complete sentences.

Are you steering your ship or are you a victim to the ill or fair winds of fate? Are you a puppet dangling from the strings of your heredity and environment? Are there a lot of things you have to do in life that have been forced upon you? Do you have to eat? No, you could starve if you chose to! You eat because you want to, because you've decided to, because it's profitable to your body. People who feel they have to do things usually forfeit many available options and alternatives and lose control of their lives in the bargain.

Responsible Self-Control

Positive Self-Control is the path to mental health and, frequently, to physical health as well. Research in biofeedback and meditation has verified human potential for control of brain wave emissions and body functions through specialized training and discipline. It is possible and may be practical for us to control our brain wave frequencies, pulse rate, threshold of pain, and other body functions as a means of positive health maintenance in the future.

There are biofeedback clinics in various parts of the country teaching people how to raise their body temperatures in their finger-tips in order to prevent the onset of migraine headaches; how to dilate their arteries to permit a greater blood flow to the heart; and how to relax muscles and nerve endings.

There also has been a remarkable breakthrough in psychology, which was first led by Abraham Maslow prior to his death, and by Carl Rodgers, William Glasser, Viktor Frankl, and many other prominent humanists and psychologists. This movement, which is optimistic about human growth and potential, is commonly referred to as *Responsibility Psychology*. It holds that irresponsibility and valuelessness lead to abnormal behavior, neuroses, and mental deterioration. Treatment for individuals suffering from these symptoms includes showing them that they need not be hung up on the past but are responsible for their present actions as well as their future behavior. Psychiatrist Glasser and others have found that, when the neurotic individual is helped to assume personal responsibility, the prognosis for recovery is good. In case after case, they verify that responsible self-control leads to sound mental health.

Life Is Choice

The winning human being realizes that everything in life is choice – even being alive. You don't have to work, go to school, eat, or even get up in the morning. You decide to do things because they are profitable to you and the best choice among the alternatives available to help you along toward your goals. People who *have* to do things are not responsible. They are not in control. They are puppets caught in the habit of letting life happen to them. Winners make things happen.

In his book, *Self-Renewal*, John Gardner states that winning individuals do not leave the development of their potential to chance; they pursue it systematically. Daily, thousands of individuals are demonstrating Gardner's statement that *"We don't know that we've been imprisoned until we've broken out."* We are not only the victims of habit. In a very real sense each of us becomes a prisoner of hundreds of restrictions of our own making. Those who refuse to be responsible for their own deeds, looking to others for their behavior cues, have not reached responsible maturity. Unfortunately, many adults spend their entire lives at this level of immaturity.

Do We Limit Ourselves?

As we grow into adulthood, we make decisions that progressively narrow our opportunities and alternatives. We select only a few friends out of the many with whom we rub elbows, usually people with whom we agree, thus limiting our received input of fresh ideas. We choose our educational level which in turn determines to a great extent our jobs and associates. From day to day, comfortable in our safe, established ways, we seek the paths of least resistance. Famed anthropologist Margaret Mead called personal responsibility our most important evolution, and the notion that we are the product of our environment our biggest sin. The responsible people look at the shackles they have placed upon themselves by apathy and lack of imagination and, in a moment of truth, decry their predicament. Making a declaration of independence, they assert their option to choose and assume their rightful role of **personal responsibility** which allows them to be true to themselves while making the best use of their minds, talents, and time.

Cause and Effect

Motivationalist Earl Nightingale has reminded us through the years of one of the great natural laws of the universe: The **Law of Cause and Effect**. For every cause, there will be an effect nearly equal in intensity. If we make good use of our minds, skills, and talents, this will become illustrated in our outer lives. And, if we make the best use of our time, this too will give us a great advantage – for we know that scarcely one in a thousand individuals ever puts his or her time to anywhere near its potential good use. This is being true to ourselves – taking control, accepting responsibility. In the final analysis, we are the only ones from whom we can steal time, talent, and accomplishment. We are the only true field judges in our own daily Superbowls in Life.

There should be a Statue of Responsibility to match the Statue of Liberty. The inscription for all to see could fittingly be these words from *My Creed* by Dean Alfange:

> *I do not choose to be a common man or woman.*
> *It is my right to be uncommon – if I can.*
> *I seek opportunity – not security.*
> *I do not wish to be a kept citizen,*
> *humbled and dulled by having the state look after me.*
> *I want to take the calculated risk –*
> *to dream and build – to fail and succeed.*
> *I refuse to barter incentive for a dole.*
> *I prefer the challenges of life to*
> *the guaranteed existence – the thrill of fulfillment to*
> *the calm state of Utopia.*
> *I will not trade freedom for beneficence*
> *– nor my dignity for a handout.*
> *I will never cower before any master*
> *– nor bend to any threat.*
> *It is my heritage to stand erect, proud and unafraid –*
> *to think and act for myself – enjoy the benefits of my*
> *creations and to face the world boldly, and say –*
> *This I have done.*

Without individual self-control and responsibility there can be no enduring liberty or freedom in our society. We will be free only as long as we can use freedom responsibly. Winners get behind the wheel, firmly in the drivers' seat. Winners take control of their thoughts, their daily routines, their goals, and their lives. They create their own horoscopes and astrological forecasts. *Winners spend their time Winning.*

REVIEW

Read this Positive Self-Control Review several times over a period of one month to etch it in your memory.

The *Positive Self-Control* of a *Total Winner* is accepting complete responsibility for causing the effects in his or her life. *Winners* realize that they have the power to take control of many more aspects of their lives, both mental and physical, than were thought possible. They know that self-control is the key to both mental and physical health and can contribute enormously to total well-being. *Losers* say: *"I can't understand why life did this to me."* *Winners* say: *"I take the credit or the blame for my performance."*

Take the credit for determining, creating, and making your own place in this world, not biorhythm computers, astrological signs, or any other outside influences. You're in the driver's seat in your own life. In many respects, you've exerted control since you were born. You can learn how to respond and adapt more successfully to the stresses of life by accepting responsibility today for causing your own effects. You alone hold the key to your reactions to people who want to rain on your parade. Remember, it's not so much *"what happens"* that counts in life; it's *"how you take it."* The real essence of *Positive Self-Control* is that everything in life is volitional and that each of us has many more choices and alternatives than we are willing to consider. *Winners really do make it happen for themselves.*

Thought-Provoking Questions

1. How much control do you have over your own life? What innate and environmental factors influence us? Why and to what degree do we allow this?

2. In the Chinese language, the symbol for crisis is the combination of "danger" and "opportunity." What impending crisis or opportunity exists in your life that would benefit from your *Positive Self-Control*? What is your choice?

3. You can learn how to respond to the stresses in life by accepting responsibility for causing your own consequences. What responses and devices have you developed to deal with the stresses in your life? What are the results?

4. Discuss how accepting personal responsibility can influence your life and career.

    ❖ Many people refuse to practice *Positive Self-Control*. They don't make decisions, fearing what will happen if something goes wrong. They hold back, blaming circumstances, other people, and events for their reluctance to act. What would happen in your school, company, or organization if everyone started to accept personal responsibility for their situations? What can you do to start this trend?

    ❖ When things go wrong or problems occur, the person with *Positive Self-Control* says, "I'll accept the responsibility for the mistake I made." Losers in life say, "I don't know why this happened. It must have been (*such and such*) or (*so and so*)." How do you feel about someone who admits making a mistake?

    ❖ In what ways can you start using *Positive Self-Control* in your daily life?

Strategies for Achieving Positive Self-Control

1. Take the credit and the blame for your position in life honestly and openly.

    ❖ What do you take credit for:

    School   _____

    Family   _____

    Yourself _____

    Society _____

    Other   _____

    ❖ What do you take blame for:

    School   _____

    Family   _____

    Yourself _____

    Society _____

    Other   _____

2. Choose:

    ❖ "I've decided to" _____

    (instead of *"I have to"*)

    ❖ "I'm more comfortable doing this"

    _____

    (instead of *"I'm afraid to do that."*)

3. Set a specific time each week, preferably each day, to initiate action letters and action calls in your own behalf.

❖ Call a friend from whom you haven't heard in a while. Do something you have been meaning to do for a long time. Do it now!

❖ Don't wait for invitations to succeed – you'll go down in history as one of the almost-made-its. Go for it! If someone has not responded to a letter or request from you within two weeks, send a follow-up letter or call. If there is still no response, take an alternate approach with someone else.

I will call _____

I will do _____

4. Action TNT – Action Today Not Tomorrow

❖ Carry this motto around with you and make it part of your lifestyle.

5. Create your own best horoscope on paper.

6. For the next 30 days, go all out in your schoolwork

❖ Remember, only you can take the initiative to give your schoolwork what it has deserved all along. Dedicate yourself for just one month to giving maximum effort to your studies. At the end of that time, you'll find yourself renewing your dedication for another month.

7. Set your alarm a half-hour early tomorrow and leave it at the earlier setting.

❖ Use this extra half-hour of your life to wake up and live. Use this time to answer the questions: How can I best spend my time on priorities that are important to me?

9

POSITIVE SELF-EXPECTANCY

*That which you fear or
expect most will surely
come to pass
The body manifests what
the mind harbors*

Things usually work out my
way because I create my
daily horoscope out of my
great expectations

AIMS

❖   To utilize *Positive Self-Expectancy* as a self-management skill

❖   To identify reasons *Winners* expect to win and apply those reasons to the development of *Positive Self-Expectancy*

❖   To develop *Positive Self-Expectancy* through the use of optimism and positive thinking

❖   To write a self-fulfilling prophecy and assess the scope of desire, control, and preparation needed to realize this prediction

VOCABULARY

Positive Self-Expectancy	*Psychosomatic Medicine*
Self-Expectancy	*Endorphins*
Luck	*Optimism*

Positive Self-Expectancy is pure and simple optimism in the face of all odds. It is the single most outwardly identifiable trait demonstrated by a winning human being and is synonymous with commitment, purpose, faith, obsession, and desire. Self-Expectancy is a self-fulfilling prophecy allowing you to anticipate the best and cause it to happen. It is the idea that what you fear or expect most will likely come to pass; the body manifests what the mind harbors. *Positive Self-Expectancy* is an integral part of motivation. It begins where self-image leaves off. It takes the words, pictures, and emotions of imagination, and fuses them into energy and action by commitment.

Every Winner can be identified easily because of his or her *Positive Self-Expectancy*. Winners expect to win. They know that luck, that force which brings prosperity or success through chance or good fortune, may also be affected by the intersection of preparation and opportunity. They look at life as a very real game, not as a gamble. They expect to win for three key reasons:

1 Desire   *They want to win.*
2 Self-control   *They can make it happen.*
3 Preparation   *They are ready to win.*

If an individual is not prepared, he or she simply does not see or take advantage of a situation. Opportunities are always around, but only those who are prepared utilize them effectively. Winners seem to be lucky because their *Positive Self-Expectancy* enables them to be better prepared for their opportunities.

The Winners in sports expect the best possible outcome in their particular event. The Winner sincerely believes that he or she is among the best, and all resultant energies are focused on proving it. Doubters don't win. Winners don't doubt. Mark Spitz expected seven gold medals. Seven times during the Twentieth Summer Olympics he propelled himself through the water in his special swimming events. Incredibly, seven times he broke the existing world record. *Before* the games he exhibited a confident manner and predictions of victory. His results were the ultimate in *Positive Self-Expectancy*.

Every individual tends to receive what he or she expects in the long run. You may or may not get what is coming to you, or you may or

Self-Expectancy

may not get what you deserve – but you will nearly always get what you expect. Losers generally expect such occurrences as the loss of a job, bankruptcy, a dull evening, bad service, failure, and even ill health. Winners, on the other hand, expect to succeed, have financial security, and enjoy good health and happy personal relationships.

Mind/Body Relationships

Careful studies of the life histories of thousands of widely differing people have persuaded competent scientists that "health changes" such as sickness or accident may be predicted. This finding is one of the many results of research in **psychosomatic medicine** – the study of the relationship between the mind and the body and how each affects the other. Scientists are learning that disease may also be linked to the ways individuals react to life.

Along with the relationship between stressful life changes and expectant anxiety, health changes seem to be associated with the body's immunity system, which makes antibodies to fight foreign material and germs. Situations which arouse fear and anxiety also suppress many body functions and may suppress antibody production as well. Distressful situations may also upset the production of hormones which have a role in emotional balance. An emotionally upset individual is much more prone to accidents. So too, a condition such as ulcers may be the result of stress rather than improper nutrition.

Dr. Herbert Benson, Associate Professor of Medicine at Harvard Medical School and Director of the Division of Behavioral Medicine at Boston's Beth Israel Hospital, is a well-known authority on the self-expectancy relationship between the mind and the body. He is the author of the *Relaxation Response* and *The Mind/Body Effect*, which document the relationship of emotions to many diseases. In *The Mind/Body Effect*, Benson explains the close interrelation between the mind and body in which thought processes lead both to disease and to good health. The concept of "Voodoo Death" is the extreme example of the potential negative effects of the mind on the body.

One documented example in Dr. Benson's book tells of a young aborigine who, during a journey, slept at an older friend's home. For breakfast, the friend had prepared a meal consisting of wild hen, a food which the young were strictly prohibited from eating. The young man demanded to know whether the meal consisted of wild hen and the host responded "No." The young man then ate the meal and departed. Several years later, when the two friends met again, the older man asked his friend whether he would now eat a wild hen. The young man said he would not since he had been solemnly ordered not to do so by his elder tribesmen. The older man laughed and told him how he had been previously tricked into eating this forbidden food. The young man became extremely frightened and started to tremble. Within twenty-four hours he was dead!

Consider, also, the death of Elvis Presley, the rock-and-roll legend. He died shortly before his forty-third birthday, just as did his mother. It has been rumored that Presley said he would die at the same age as his mother. Although there has been much discussion as to the effect of the drugs that were involved, one of the least mentioned, more interesting aspects of Elvis Presley's death is that he may have been obsessed with it during the last year of his life and he probably expected it to happen.

Today, support groups for cancer patients often provide not only comfort but an environment that breeds a positive attitude for the possibility of remission. Doctors often comment, and not without reason, that a patient's "attitude" can be a key element in his or her recovery. Research has yet to substantiate the notion that "thinking well" will make you well but there are thousands of active, former open-heart surgery patients who are proof positive that their outlook toward total recovery made all the difference.

The Drug of Optimism

Discoveries about the brain relate directly to the theory of why optimism is one of the single most important traits in a winning human being. These discoveries reveal that the body produces morphine-like proteins called **endorphins**. These naturally produced substances may reduce the experience of pain and also cause the organism to feel better. The discovery of these internal opiates, secreted and used by the brain, may be the beginning of a break-through to understanding joy and depression. Presumably, these natural substances help people screen out unpleasant stimuli.

In his book, *Optimism: The Biology of Hope*, Dr. Lionel Tiger makes a strong case for the possibility of a location in the brain that creates good feelings about the present and the future. Dr. Tiger suggests that we have developed this capability in our internal pharmacy ever since prehistoric times, when, as hunters, we optimistically entertained the idea of the successful hunt.

He suggests that people who are pessimistic or depressed may use external stimuli to cure their depression. These stimuli can run the gamut from huge doses of vitamins, drugs, or alcohol to extravagant shopping sprees, vacations, or sessions with psychiatrists. Conversely, optimistic self-expectancy creates a natural high to help winners withstand pain, overcome depression, turn stress into energy, and persist.

What does all this have to do with self-expectancy and winning attitudes? Simply this: Mental obsessions have physical manifestations. You become that which you fear, you get what you expect, you are that which you expect to be. The power of the self-fulfilling prophecy is one of the most amazing phenomena of human nature. The Winner in life, believing in the self-fulfilling prophecy, keeps his or her momentum upward by expecting a better job, good health, financial gain, warm friendships, and success. The Winner sees problems as opportunities to challenge ability and determination. Winners use **optimism** (*the ability to look for the positives in all situations*) to fulfill their own prophecies.

Optimistic Winning

Since all individuals are responsible for their own actions and cause their own effects, optimism is a choice. Achieving individuals, Winners, are "self-made," since their positive expectations make them what they are. People shy away from negative, pessimistic, unbelieving Losers. They gravitate to positive, self-assured, optimistic Winners.

Positive Self-Expectancy is important for all of us no matter what our profession. The enthusiasm of optimistic people is contagious. In their presence no one can remain neutral or indifferent. Their gentle good humor and ability to look on the bright side of life establishes an *esprit de corps* with those around them. The winning individual knows that an attitude of optimistic expectancy is the surest way to create an upward cycle and to attract the best of "luck" most of the time.

When people ask you why you're always so enthusiastic about life, tell them you're on the drug of optimism, which keeps you going toward the next decade. Tell them it flows naturally and freely from within, as a primary ingredient for winning. Optimism is like a forest fire; you can smell it for miles before you see it burning. Optimism is like flypaper. You can't help getting stuck to it. Everybody loves a Winner. No one seems to swarm around a consistent Loser. Optimism. Enthusiasm. Each is a synonym for *Positive Self-Expectancy*.

What do you expect for yourself? The Winner in life, believing in the self-fulfilling prophecy, keeps his or her momentum moving upward by expecting a better job, good health, financial gain, warm friendships, and success. The Winners see problems as opportunities to challenge their ability and determination. What can you expect for yourself in life if not to Win? *Expect to Win.*

REVIEW

Read this Positive Self-Expectancy Review several times over the period of one month to etch it in your memory.

The most readily identifiable quality of a total *Winner* is an overall attitude of personal optimism and enthusiasm. *Winners* understand the relationship between mind and body. The body expresses the mind's thoughts. They know that life is a self-fulfilling prophecy, that a person usually gets what he or she actively expects. *Losers* say, *"With my luck, I was bound to fail." Winners* say: *"I was good today, I'll be better tomorrow."*

Your fears and worries can turn into anxiety, which is distressing to your body. You may become more vulnerable to disease and accident. Conversely, if your mental expectancy is healthy, your body will seek to display this general feeling with better health, energy, and a condition of well-being. By expecting the best as a way of life, you are preparing yourself physically as well as mentally for the demands of winning.

Thought-Provoking Questions

1. What do you desire? What do you do to control the outcome? Are you prepared? If so, how? What have you done? What opportunities have you taken?

2. Armed with an understanding of the "psychosomatic" phenomenon, how have you unknowingly applied it in the past and what opportunities do you see for its use in the future?

3. If you are what you expect, what prevents a Loser from becoming a Winner? Is this destiny?

4. If you become that which you fear and that which you expect to be, how can you prevent "bad luck" or obstacles from overtaking you?

5. What will you do to develop a sense of humor; to laugh more often and to generate enthusiasm and optimism around the people with whom you associate?

6. What are your strongest beliefs? What do you value most? How do these beliefs and values affect your optimism and outlook on the future?

Strategies for Achieving Self-Expectancy

1. Use positive self-talk every day.

    It's another good day for me
    Things usually work out my way
    I expect a great day
    Next time I'll do better
    I'll make it

2. Identify the good in all your personal relationships.

Family	What is good about this relationship?
_____	_____
_____	_____
_____	_____
_____	_____
_____	_____
Friends	
_____	_____
_____	_____
_____	_____
_____	_____
Business Associates	
_____	_____
_____	_____
_____	_____
_____	_____

3. Look at problems as opportunities.

   ❖ List your most pressing problems in the space provided. Identify those that block your personal and professional fulfillment.

   ❖ Write a one-sentence definition of the problem. Ask yourself this question: "Why is this a problem?"

   ❖ Now change your attitude toward this problem. Look at it as an opportunity, an exercise to challenge your creativity and ingenuity. View the situation as if you were advising your best friend. Write down this exciting new opportunity.

1. *Problem* _____
   Definition _____
   Opportunity _____

2. *Problem* _____
   Definition _____
   Opportunity _____

3. *Problem* _____
   Definition _____
   Opportunity _____

4. *Problem* _____
   Definition _____
   Opportunity _____

5. *Problem* _____
   Definition _____
   Opportunity _____

EXAMPLE:

Problem: My boss doesn't appreciate all the good things I do and always points out the bad things to me.

Definition: The boss sees only the negative.

Opportunity: When my boss points out the negatives, I will use my creative mind to focus on the positives of the situation rather than defending the negatives.

4. The best way to remain optimistic is to associate with *Winners* and optimists.

   ❖ You can be realistic and optimistic at the same time by realistically examining the facts in a situation while remaining optimistic about your ability to contribute to a solution or a constructive alternative.

5. Expect the best from others, too.

   ❖ Two of the keys to leadership are encouragement and praise. Vocalize, on a daily basis, your optimism and positive expectancy about everyone in your life. It's contagious!

10

POSITIVE *SELF-DIMENSION*

If I can help you win,
then I win
If nature wins,
everyone wins

*You are best to
yourself when you
are good to others*

AIMS

❖ To integrate all aspects of *Positive Self-Dimension* into the Total Person

❖ To implement the Double Win Attitude in your life

❖ To identify the components of *Positive Self-Dimension* and assess their effects on your life

❖ To recognize symptoms of procrastination and devise ways to overcome it

❖ To design your own philosophy for life as it relates to the ten qualities presented in this textbook

VOCABULARY

Positive Self-Dimension   *Time Encounter*

Total Person   *Someday Philosophy*

Double Win Attitude   *Procrastination*

The real Winners in the game of life have **Positive Self-Dimension**. This quality enables them to lead a well-balanced life and to look beyond themselves for meaning. The goal fulfillment is that of a **Total Person**, one who is part of the big picture; knows him or herself intimately; sees through the eyes of others; feels one with nature and the universe; learns to be aware of time and opportunity and lives as fully as possible in the present.

The greatest example of self-dimension a Winner can display is the quality of earning the love and respect of other human beings. *Positive Self-Dimension* does not mean standing victoriously over a fallen enemy. *Positive Self-Dimension* is extending a strong hand to one who is reaching, or groping, or just trying to hang on. Winners create other Winners without exploiting them. They know that true immortality for the human race is when a caring, sharing person helps even one other individual to live a better life.

Self-dimension starts with the inner circle – the family. Is your family a winning team? Are your relationships valuable? Have you lost touch except for holidays, anniversaries, reunions, and parties? Winners get it together with their loved ones, their friends, and with the community in which they live. They also love their careers, but are not married to them. Winners vote and care about the government of their cities, states, nation, and the world. They are interested in its effectiveness, fairness, and honesty. Winners live a well-rounded life. They build their spheres of relationships with evenly distributed emphasis. Winners practice the **Double Win Attitude**. "If I help you win, then I win, too."

The Double Win

Self-dimension goes beyond relationships with other human beings. It applies very definitely to an individual's relationship with nature. Loving and respecting creation, winners realize that though nature is abundant, it is also unforgiving. If we exploit its resources, it responds like a mirror, reflecting our gluttony and plunder with dwindling resources, unclean air, unsafe water, and toxic food. As we change our environment to suit our short-range ambitions, we then risk the very survival of the human race. *Positive Self-Dimension* is understanding the vulnerability of the life process and the delicate balance of ecology.

Nature

Positive Self-Dimension is being in harmony with that which shapes the entire universe. It is seeing the perfection and beauty manifested through nature and accepting the imperfection in man's attempt to reshape nature in his/her own image, to rationalize his/her ignorance of the wisdom and intelligence behind the creation of life. Winners are able to put their own being in dimension with other human beings who came before, and are open to the idea that other forms of life, possibly more advanced, may be present in the outer regions of infinity.

Time

When we were children, time stood still. It took forever for holidays and summer vacation to arrive. A day in grammar school seemed like a week. Our senior year in high school moved at a snail's pace. Our twenty-first birthday was always way out in the future. A Saturday at the beach lasted forever. As we matured, we came to accept that time rules each of our lives. Winners with *Positive Self-Dimension* have a keen awareness of the value of time, which once spent is gone from their lives forever. Winners seem to understand the concept of a Time Encounter.

A **Time Encounter** is a life experience in which you come face to face with the dramatic reality that there are no time-outs, no substitutions, and no replays in the game of life – and the understanding that the clock is always running. Your encounter may be a near miss on the freeway, the loss of a friend or loved one, an illness, or a visit to a hospital. Your encounter may be as subtle as a high school class reunion, or the discovery of old photographs of you and your family. It may be the chance meeting of an "old" friend. Your encounter may be an innocent glance in the mirror.

Winners learn from these experiences and develop a cherished respect for the value of time. Losers begin to fear the passing of time, chasing it, squandering it, and, most of all, trying to hide from it, often from beneath a superficial cosmetic veil. Winners understand the mortality of their bodies and are able to age gracefully as a result. They tend their "gardens" like sensitive horticulturists instead of one-shot profit planters. They do not necessarily accept death as the final gun in the game of life. They see it as a transition into another plane which, although they may never come to fully comprehend its meaning while living, they do not fear.

Winners take time

- ❖ *to look at the rosebuds opening each day.*

- ❖ *to listen, knowing there may be fewer robins next spring.*

- ❖ *for children, who too soon fly like arrows from the bow.*

- ❖ *to play, knowing that children grow up.*

- ❖ *for older people, knowing that older often means wiser.*

- ❖ *for their families, knowing they are the inner circle of life.*

- ❖ *for nature, knowing they can't put it on their charge cards.*

- ❖ *for animals, knowing it's their world, too.*

- ❖ *to read, knowing that books are a transport of wisdom that can take them to places never imagined.*

- ❖ *to work, knowing they can't enjoy the view unless they climb the mountain.*

- ❖ *for their health, knowing it's a precious commodity.*

Someday Philosophy

Winners don't live their lives in the past; they learn from it, not repeating their mistakes but savoring each memory that brought them happiness. Winners don't live their lives in the distant future, safely out of sight according to the "**Someday Philosophy** ." Rather, they set goals in the specific, foreseeable future which give their everyday activities richness and purpose.

One of the problems shared most frequently by unhappy people is that they allow their lives to be governed by what may happen tomorrow. They are always waiting for some incident to come about in the future to make them happy: when they get married; when they complete their education; when they make more money; when they get a new car; when they complete some task, pay some bill, or overcome some difficulty. They are continually let down and frustrated. If the condition of being happy is not experienced and related to the present time, it will not be experienced at all. You cannot base happiness on an uncertain event or possible occurrence. Another problem will always come along just as you find the answer to the previous one. Your whole life is a connecting succession of difficulties and problems, both large and small, which to the Winners become no more than opportunities for challenge and growth. The only time for happiness is right now.

Procrastination, which is the intentional delay of doing what should be done, is also the fear of success. People procrastinate because they are afraid that they don't deserve the success that they know will result if they move ahead now. Because success is heavy, carries a responsibility with it, and requires an individual to continue to set an example, it is much easier to procrastinate and live on the *Someday Philosophy*.

Do It Now!

True *Positive Self-Dimension* is to live every minute as if it were your last – to always look for good – and to cherish the minutes and the lives that you encounter within it. Winners live in the present, in that only moment of time over which they have any control – now. Losers should run a classified ad in the newspaper under Lost and Found: "Lost – one twenty-four hour, twenty-four carat, golden day – each hour studded with sixty diamond minutes – each minute studded with sixty ruby seconds. But don't bother to look for it, it's gone forever – that wonderful, golden day, I lost today." Life is not a race to see who comes in first, but who comes in best.

The true Winners see their total person in such a fully-formed perspective that they literally become part of the big picture of life – and it of them. They have learned to know themselves intimately. They have learned to see themselves through the eyes of others. They have learned to feel one with nature and the universe. They have learned to be aware of time, their opportunity to learn from the past, plan for the future, and live as fully as possible in the present. *For each of us, the clock is running and there is still plenty of time to Win!*

REVIEW

Read this Positive Self-Dimension Review several times over the period of one month to etch it in your memory.

Winners see their total person in such a fully-formed perspective that they literally become part of the "big picture" of life – and it of them. They have learned to know themselves intimately. They have learned to see themselves through the eyes of others. They have learned to feel as one with nature and the universe. And they have learned to be aware of time – their opportunity to learn from the past, plan for the future, and live as fully as possible in the present. *Winners* create other *Winners* without exploiting them. They get it together with their loved ones, their friends, and with the community in which they live. They practice the Double-Win Attitude: "If I help you win, then I win."

Positive Self-Dimension is understanding the vulnerability of the life process and the delicate balance of ecology. *Winners* understand the mortality of their bodies and as a result are able to age gracefully. They do not necessarily accept death as the final gun in the game of life. They see it as a transition which, although they may never come to fully comprehend its meaning, they do not fear; they anticipate its eventual arrival. *Winners* plant shade trees under which they know they'll never sit. A *Winner*'s self-talk: "*I live every moment, enjoying as much, relating as much, doing as much, giving as much as I possibly can.*"

Thought-Provoking Questions

1. In the past, have you encountered the Double Win Attitude? Explain the situation. What were the results? In what situation could you be responsible for fostering a Double Win?

2. What do you see in the mirror? Describe your dimension as it relates to nature, harmony, animals, and time.

3. If today were your last day, what would you do? Why? Why or why not live each day as if it were your last?

4. What does *Positive Self-Dimension* start with? What do you need to do to get started?

5. In Positive Self-Direction, you examined eight areas of your life and set short and long-term goals in each area. Have you been making plans and taking action to reach those goals? As you look at your "Game Plan for Life," which area is your largest priority now? Are there any areas you wish to emphasize? How does having a well-balanced life directly relate to *Positive Self-Dimension*?

6. Are you a success? By what standards do you measure success? Whose expectations do you feel compelled to fulfill? Why?

7. What type of relationships do you aspire to build in your own world of *Positive Self-Dimension*? What components are needed for construction?

Strategies for Achieving Self-Dimension

As a final project, compose your "Philosophy of Life" using the following guidelines. Record it in a journal or write it as an essay.

❖   Start with an introduction of who you are: How do you fit into your family? school? career?

❖   Include the first nine qualities presented in this textbook and expand upon your understanding and use of each and how they fit into your "Philosophy of Life."

❖   Conclude with a discussion of your fit into this world through the tenth quality, *Positive Self-Dimension.*

GLOSSARY

Active Listening ❖ Taking responsibility for what is heard; asking questions, requesting examples, or paraphrasing for clarity and understanding; *Chapter 7*

Adaptability ❖ Remaining open and flexible to the actions of others through empathy and self-awareness; *Chapter 5*

Conscious Mind ❖ *(The Judge)* Upper level of mental thought characterized by sensation, emotion, and volition; *Chapter 2*

Current Dominant Thought ❖ The concept that says we tend to move toward the things we think about most; *Chapter 4*

Desire ❖ A powerful motivating emotion which attracts, opens , directs, and encourages plans and goals; a strong, positive magnet; *Chapter 3*

Distress ❖ Negative stress; *Chapter 5*

Double Win Attitude ❖ Getting what you want out of life by helping others get what they want; "If I help you win, then I win, too!"; *Chapter 10*

Emotions ❖ Automatic subconscious reactions; *Chapter 6*

Empathy ❖ The understanding, awareness, and sensitivity of the feelings, thoughts, and experiences of another in a vicarious way; *Chapter 5*

Encode ❖ Converting one form of communication to another; *Chapter 7*

Endorphins ❖ Proteins which occur naturally in the brain; may reduce the experience of pain; *Chapter 9*

Environmental Self-Awareness ❖ Sensitivity and understanding of one's surroundings, the needs of others, and one's personal involvement with life; *Chapter 5*

Esteem ❖ To appreciate value or worth; *Chapter 6*

Fear ❖ Negative motivating emotion which restricts plans and defeats goals; *Chapter 4*

Fight or Flight ❖ The body's automatic decision-making response to a life or death situation whereby a person will defend him/herself or flee; *Chapter 5*

Goal ❖ The desired outcome toward which all effort is directed; *Chapter 1*

Habits ❖ Behavior patterns that have been acquired through frequent repetition and have become involuntary; can control everyday life; *Chapter 3*

Happiness ❖ State of well-being and contentment; natural by-product of a worthwhile life; *Chapter 1*

Imagination ❖ Creating mental images of things not present in reality; the greatest tool in the universe; *Chapter 2*

Imagineering ❖ Taking ideas and developing them into reality; *Chapter 2*

Invisible Entrapment ❖ A syndrome manifested by the deep-seated worries, frustrations, and anxieties of people unable to cope effectively with their changing status in a changing world; *Chapter 5*

Judge ❖ *See Conscious Mind; Chapter 2*

Law of Cause and Effect ❖ For every cause there will be an effect nearly equal in intensity; *Chapter 8*

Life-Controlling Mechanism ❖ The self-image which determines the kind and scope of person we are; *Chapter 2*

Losers ❖ People who wander aimlessly through life or self-destruct; *Chapter 1*

Luck ❖ Force which brings prosperity or success through chance or good fortune; may be affected by the intersection of preparation and opportunity; *Chapter 9*

Mental Self-Awareness ❖ Knowledge of the potential and abundance within our minds which waits to be challenged; *Chapter 5*

Motivation ❖ Force which springs from inside an individual and moves him/her to action; *Chapter 4*

Motive ❖ An idea, need, emotion, or desire which incites action; *Chapter 4*

Nonverbal Communication ❖ Communicating through body actions rather than through words; sending intentions and feelings through nonverbal signals; *Chapter 7*

Optimism ❖ The ability to look for the positives in all situations; *Chapter 9*

Permanent Potential ❖ Untapped ability for sustained success; *Chapter 6*

Personal Responsibility ❖ Taking the responsibility for making the best use of your mind, talents, and time; being true to yourself; *Chapter 8*

Physical Self-Awareness ❖ Taking good care of your body and being aware that when you feel good, you look good, do good, and perform better; *Chapter 5*

Positive Self-Awareness ❖ The ability to step back and take a good look at yourself as you relate to your environmental, physical, and mental world; acceptance of yourself as a unique, imperfect, changing, and growing individual with potential; *Chapter 5*

Positive Self-Control ❖ Taking full responsibility for determining your actions; choosing your own destinies; *Chapter 8*

Positive Self-Dimension ❖ The quality of a whole, total, well-rounded person who is leading a well-balanced life; the ability to look beyond oneself for the meaning of life; *Chapter 10*

Positive Self-Direction ❖ Establishing a clearly defined goal and acting on it; *Chapter 1*

Positive Self-Discipline ❖ Mental practice from within to make or break habits, change self-image, or achieve goals; *Chapter 3*

Positive Self-Esteem ❖ Accepting yourself the way you are at this moment; the ability to base actions and decisions on rational thinking, rather than emotion; leads to achievement and happiness; *Chapter 6*

Positive Self-Expectancy ❖ Pure and simple optimism charged by faith, commitment, purpose, obsession, or desire; *Chapter 9*

Positive Self-Image ❖ Taking one's self-concept and empowering it to make you the person you want to be; *Chapter 2*

Positive Self-Motivation ❖ The force that moves one in the direction of personally set goals; an inner drive to move upward toward self-fulfillment; *Chapter 4*

Positive Self-Projection ❖ Having an aura of success and confidence projected by strong communication skills and a good appearance; *Chapter 7*

Positive Self-Talk ❖ Mental dialogue with yourself in order to effect positive results; *Chapter 3*

Positive Tension ❖ An inner striving or unrest often manifested by a physiological indication of emotion; *Chapter 4*

Procrastination ❖ The intentional delay of doing what should be done; fear of success; *Chapter 10*

Psychosomatic Medicine ❖ The study of the relationship between the mind and the body and how each affects the other; *Chapter 9*

Racehorses ❖ Characterization of one who needs to race on to win and cannot be confined or corralled; *Chapter 5*

Receiver ❖ One who receives messages from a sender and encodes them; *Chapter 7*

Repetition ❖ The technique of practicing over and over through self-talk or imagination; *Chapter 3*

Robot ❖ *See Subconscious Mind; Chapter 2*

Self-Acceptance ❖ The willingness to be yourself and live your life as it is unfolding; *Chapter 6*

Self-Esteem ❖ Confidence and satisfaction in one's self; *Chapter 6*

Self-Expectancy ❖ Self-fulfilling prophecy; anticipating the best and causing it to happen; *Chapter 9*

Self-Image ❖ Concept of self; *Chapter 2*

Self-Molded ❖ Shaping your destinies through your own actions; *Chapter 8*

Sender ❖ One who telegraphs intentions and feelings; *Chapter 7*

Simulation ❖ Creating and practicing experiences in your mind; *Chapter 3*

Social Slights ❖ Offending remarks or actions, intentional or not, that occur publicly; *Chapter 6*

Someday Philosophy ❖ Living life in the distant future; waiting for some event that might happen; *Chapter 10*

Stress ❖ A physical, chemical, or emotional effect that causes bodily or mental tension and may be a factor in disease causation; *Chapter 5*

Subconscious Mind ❖ *(The Robot)* That part of the mind which controls mental activities just below the threshold of consciousness; *Chapter 2*

Success ❖ The progressive realization of goals that are worthy of the individual; *Chapter 1*

Time Encounter ❖ A life experience in which you come face to face with the reality that time never stops; *Chapter 10*

Total Person ❖ Someone who is part of the big picture of life, knows themselves intimately, sees through the eyes of others, feels one with nature and the universe, learns to be aware of time and opportunity, and lives as fully as possible in the present, *Chapter 10*

Turtles ❖ Characterization of one who cannot, or should not, be forced to move too fast for his or her own unique step-by-step nature; *Chapter 5*

Winners ❖ Individuals who get what they want from life; they set and achieve goals that benefit others as well as themselves; *Chapter 1*

Winner's Circle ❖ Area where Winners with Positive Self-Image mentally visualize themselves attaining the goals they set; *Chapter 2*

Winner's Edge ❖ The fine line between the top five percent of the real achievers (*Winners*) in society and everyone else; *Chapter 4*

Winning Self-Direction ❖ Setting goals that are realistic and meaningful to you; *Chapter 1*

Winning ❖ Taking the talent or potential you were born with and have since developed and using it fully toward a purpose that makes you feel worthwhile according to your own internal standards; *Chapter 1*

Notes